T0067501

Enchanting
Shaula Pearl

Joy Is for All Souls

Geila Jones

BALBOA.
PRESS
A DIVISION OF HAY HOUSE

Copyright © 2015 Geila Jones.

All rights reserved. No part of this book may be used or reproduced by any means, graphic, electronic, or mechanical, including photocopying, recording, taping or by any information storage retrieval system without the written permission of the publisher except in the case of brief quotations embodied in critical articles and reviews.

Balboa Press books may be ordered through booksellers or by contacting:

Balboa Press
A Division of Hay House
1663 Liberty Drive
Bloomington, IN 47403
www.balboapress.com
1 (877) 407-4847

Because of the dynamic nature of the Internet, any web addresses or links contained in this book may have changed since publication and may no longer be valid. The views expressed in this work are solely those of the author and do not necessarily reflect the views of the publisher, and the publisher hereby disclaims any responsibility for them.

The author of this book does not dispense medical advice or prescribe the use of any technique as a form of treatment for physical, emotional, or medical problems without the advice of a physician, either directly or indirectly. The intent of the author is only to offer information of a general nature to help you in your quest for emotional and spiritual well-being. In the event you use any of the information in this book for yourself, which is your constitutional right, the author and the publisher assume no responsibility for your actions.

Any people depicted in stock imagery provided by Thinkstock are models, and such images are being used for illustrative purposes only.
Certain stock imagery © Thinkstock.

Print information available on the last page.

Library of Congress Control Number: 2015910676

ISBN: 978-1-5043-3598-0 (sc)
ISBN: 978-1-5043-3599-7 (e)

Balboa Press rev. date: 07/30/2015

Contents

Dedication

This book is dedicated to my lovely daughters, Rachael and Wendi,
whom I treasure beyond words, and to
the sweet soul of Shaula Pearl,
and to all animal souls who are in need of joyful enchantment.

Acknowledgements

I wish to thank Balboa Press, a division of Hay House Publishing, and all those involved in this project, and to Virginia Morell, Barbara Carter, and Mary Wegener, my angel team, who gave me exceptional support and guidance, making my vision of this book manifest.

I would like to offer a special thank you to Louise Hay, founder of Hay House, for her joy inspired visions, providing me and numerous others with a safe place to harvest our dreams and share our journeys.

Also, a warm thank you to Michael Kwiecinski for his passionate dedication to this project and his intuitive and expert skill in preparing the photography for this book. He pulled out the goddess in Shaula Pearl, giving her the courage to pose and show her sweet spirit.

To my granddaughter Jasmyne who inspires me.
To my niece Chelsea, my late night writing buddy.

Prologue to Enchantment

Flowers are innately inspired to blossom. Rain falls gently, bejeweling spider webs. The rich, luscious colors of Autumn, setting trees on fire, enchant us without effort. The same day has a flip-side, dark and nightmarish, trembling with uncontrollable fear. Shaula Pearl's day, over and over again, until she was rescued.

Shaula Pearl's journey is frightening, flooded with deep fears. At the same time, it glows like the moon, dipped in Divine Light, joyful and passionate by nature. Glow is stronger than fear. She became brave in her own way. It took almost a year with mistakes from the human. She always forgave me, coming out of her closet, but not without boundaries. Abuse left her with painful scars, but they have shrunk significantly. The power of love transcends the most potent healing elixir on this earth, because love is what we are made of.

There is a deep and poetic beauty to life. Too many beautiful souls have no conscious awareness of it. Shaula Pearl was emotionless, mentally numb when I adopted her. By the grace of Divine Light, the seeds of enchantment - love, joy, and hope, took hold with tough roots, linking her to the sacredness of her own soul. I was fortunate. I felt the magic of being alive, since I was a young child, aware of the spiritual realms pouring into my world without warning. It gave me an exuberance for all life, for the gentle beauty of trees, for the wild souls of crows, and the placid composure of toads, plump in their own joy, sitting along the weedy shores of moss lined ponds.

As I grew older, I felt a passionate and persistent hunger to connect with spirit and to increase my perceptions beyond the appearances of this world. I was aware of my guides and angels, encouraging me to be fearless. I felt their amazing presence often and their nagging persistence to stay on track. If you get overly excited about a caterpillar, feel that all moments in life are miraculous, and hot joy throbs through your veins, it can be challenging to hold everything together. As a result, one unsuspecting morning, they shoved me into my current journey, unconcerned about my bliss-challenged mind.

The day that I adopted my sweet girl, the flood gates opened wide, submerging me in the incredible landscape of the spirit world, more than ever. Shaula Pearl stood by me, stiff-legged, afraid to move. Our journey together was divinely inspired and beyond both of our hopes. She found her soul, away from the hell that imprisoned her. I discovered what the word grace meant and how deep the well is that we pull love from, and beyond that, the radiance of the word joy, which I thought I was aware of. If there ever was a physical manifestation of the word joy, exploding out of a soul, it was Shaula Pearl. Late one night, someone with a strong foot, kicked opened a doorway, and she slipped through, claiming who she was. Her life, at that point, changed forever. So did mine.

Shaula Pearl is barely twelve now and one of the most gentlest souls I have ever known. She was six when I brought her home. It was pure chaos that day. She thought I was a monster-human. She had no idea what a house was. The stairs paralyzed her with fear. I had to wrap my arms around her belly and walk her up. I was kindly warned that she might be fear aggressive, capable of attacking me. It did occur to me, half way up the stairs, with a strange noise coming out of her throat. But at the same time, I knew she wouldn't. Spirit led me to her, and if you can't trust spirit, who can you trust?

The deal was done. The stars ignited our path. We were on it, two feet and four paws, and there was no turning back. That was my first promise to Shaula Pearl, with many more to come. I would never return her to the shelter. I would enchant her, no matter how long it took. Even when she gutted my favorite chair or ate my fake pussy willows, I didn't hesitate to remind her that I loved her, but all the dark chocolate in the house was off limits. I would share the milk chocolate. Enchantment flourishes with abundant measures of humor.

Ray Bradbury was on the enchantment plan with his warm wisdom. "We are cups, constantly and quietly being filled. The trick is, knowing how to tip ourselves over and let the beautiful stuff out." That was the challenge. I had to locate her heart key, deeply embedded in her soul, and then twist it slowly, listening for that click, opening her up to the exquisite loveliness of being alive and loved.

I had help, besides the mood enhancers of chocolate and some child development insights. The elegance and beauty of Divine Light, including my angels, guides, and deceased pets, all rallied to her side. I give them credit for their tireless guidance and encouragement daily, and often, deep into the night, inspiring us both to never give up on each other. By the end of the first year, I wasn't sure where Shaula Pearl ended and I began. Love melded us together. It holds everything together. Her painful memories still haunt her, but now she has a joy run. Everyone has the right to a joy run.

Her journey has left me gasping for enchantment. Things happened that I will never forget and that buoy my own spirit, daily. Strange and extraordinary events became normal. I offer you everything, the wild and wonderful moments of this journey, plus the more chilling ones, including all of her snuffs and gurgles, her own unique voice, unfolding slowly and delicately, wanting to be heard. She has a lot to say because no one ever listened.

As you read the text of this journey, apply your own words for Divine Light, for God and Goddess, and for the way I describe nature with male or female attributes. Use whatever deity you honor. Divine Light has many names and many paths. He-she is all the energies of this earth and dwells in all souls. Also, when you read the word dog, you can think animal or cat, bird or Guinee pig, whatever feels right.

My words are not as important as the drift of them. Let them connect you to the rich, spiritual soil where we all came from, where Shaula Pearl came from, innocent and trusting. Let them fill you with beautiful thoughts and the gentle wisdom of the earth that whispers to us, telling us what it's all about. Love. A deep and meaningful relationship with your own soul. A passionate desire to enchant the souls of others. Also, to know that a great and infinite river of joy flows through you. Dive deep. Gulp mouthfuls of it. Scoop it up. Pass it around.

Shaula Pearl is here to herald in a message, so needed now. Love one another. Help and heal all living beings. Enchant when you can. Never give up on yourself or on anyone else. Never stop believing in divine love, for the mere whisper of it travels around the earth, changing the course of storms, moving mountains, opening doorways you thought were closed or never existed - and saving souls.

Love and joy in boundless amounts to all of you,

Geila

CHAPTER ONE

DREAMS AND JOURNEYS
"You were made perfectly to be loved."
Elizabeth Barrett Browning

"The darkest night of a soul. Crushing inward. Heart, numb. Body, stiff. Eyes, ghostly. A shadowy stare, afraid to look at the monster. Me. Human. Our first day together. I committed. Love without conditions. I looked like a fool to some. A sucker for a soul. So be it." Geila the Dreamer.

"We will be friends until forever, just you wait and see." Winnie the Pooh.

Five years ago, my life changed. Nobody was aware of it until my home began to look different. Chunks of things, scattered on the carpet. Objects of art, stuffed into a closet. A bagel, half eaten, slightly green, under a sofa pillow. My gray carpet was morphing into a non-descript color, muddy like. As a result, it was covered with a wide assortment of throw blankets, including a beach towel covering exposed foam, bulging out of an arm chair. At the end of the first year, it was fair to say, that my décor was no longer candles and beach rocks with a touch of modified Goth. It was classic Shaula Pearl.

I embraced our journey together with quiet gushes of joy, because noise scared her. I was hopeful about all possible enchanted outcomes, but conscious of the polarities of life, I was ready for anything. With the humor and charm of divine intervention, I had a spiritual support team that made all the difference, tempering the heart hammering moments, substantial gulps of air and rising anxiety when I was out of chocolate.

When you find your path, it brings you the strength of a tiger, running in perfect symmetry through a forest. You dodge the brambles and the twisted roots of trees. Even so, there are days that are difficult to swallow, when you step on something unpleasant, or you discover your mattress gutted with a large piece of foam wedged in a flower vase. You don't question how or why. You forgive instantly, aware that enchantment is delicate and needs a continuous source of fuel. It runs exclusively on love and joy and your ability to grin. Practice.

Looking out of my bedroom window, in front of my writing desk, I see a very small cut of the world, framed. No matter how limited the view, it is the physical manifestation of a mind, luminous and divine. I see black, glossy crows with glints of auburn on their wings and orangey brown leaves, pirouetting down the street in a light gust of wind. To the left of my window, there is a large magnolia tree with creamy white flowers in full bloom – the simplicity of nature in all its grandeur.

Not every soul has a pleasant view. The sweet face of an animal, peering at you from out a window, lined with velvet drapes and gold cords, appears to be living an enchanted life. The deceptions of this physical world are enormous. He has nothing. Fear chokeholds the day. He waits for the kick in his side. The punch on his face.

Shaula Pearl has shattered some of the most attractive illusions, exposing the real treasures of our lives, all love-fashioned. She has shown me joy, wild and explosive. She has trusted me with her fears, making me highly conscious of what it means to care for another soul. She has taught me the power of words, more than ever. They can inflict deep cuts for a lifetime. They can flood the earth with torrential downpours of love energy, of divine energy that all souls are made of. New mantras arose overnight – the first one being window inspired. All creatures, walking on the divine soil of this earth, are worthy of a window with a lovely view, a safe home, and to feel the undercurrent of joy, spliced into every moment – and if it moves them, dream of sweet honey baked into their dog biscuits.

Shaula Pearl has a view now, devoid of bars. She has heat in the morning and a warm bed at night. She doesn't live in the nightmare anymore of her previous residence, but she has nightmares. Her memories won't leave her alone entirely. She has something to say about it, in her pre-enchanted existence. "I saw nothing, even if my eyes were open. The stars above my cage, with the scent of death around me, went unnoticed. In my world, there was only danger and decay, and there was no way out. I felt dead and so did the other dogs, packed tightly against my body, heaving and panting. I was afraid to breathe. I slept with my eyes open. I was never safe."

This was Shaula Pearl's home, or better said, her hell house. In the wildest stretch of the imagination, she was one of the more fortunate ones. Numerous dogs, where she lived, were dead and stuffed into buckets or lying on the ground, withered and cold as stone. Many of the dogs were injured, hiding under wheelbarrows or in boxes. A few hundred animals were taken from an animal hoarder, five years ago, with people going home crying, because they couldn't rescue all of them in one day.

This world is a huge womb, birthing our thoughts and dreams. She takes care of us, nourishing us daily with her divine gifts, made for all souls, and some of them very personal - heat and water, sunlight and moonlight, milk chocolate fudge or dark chocolate fondue, plus a deluge of experiences, many of them joyful, feeding the cravings of our own unique souls. At the same time, segments of our lives can be soul shredding. I collapsed in bed, thinking about all this, after my first non-enchanted week with Shaula Pearl, who had crammed herself into the back corner of a closet, stiff as wood. I felt a sadness about the way things were. Life should glow like a prism, rotating around us, dancing with us, chanting our names, filling us with moments of great luminosity at all times. Despite my personal feelings, it doesn't quite happen that way. Still, I trusted in the divinity of journeys, as harsh and frightening as they can be.

Sleep was in some other realm. It was painful to breathe, only because I could feel her fear, bleeding outward. Most likely, she was feeling me, also. I didn't want her to sense anything negative, so I did something a little odd, if only to relax. I stared at the ceiling. Small dots of light, flashing in hues of blues and greens and some silver, swirled overhead in random patterns. I had seen them since I was a young child, creating images of my dolls and stuffed animals, waving at me in mid-air. I have a friend who sees rocket ships, so maybe it's not so unusual.

There is research on dots in the dark. A physical phenomenon is a good explanation. The eye itself creates images when there is no light. It makes sense, but if you were born with a magical mind, you feel differently about many things. To me, they are the loving presence of angels and the playful energy of fairies. At the very least, they are manifestations of my own mind, flashing with inspiration. I would need them all. The coming months would prove to be some of the most exhausting and challenging moments of my life, but also the most inspiring.

Shaula Pearl had no awareness of the waves of joy, churning around the corners of the universe, flowing her way. For the moment, she was stuck in a place where darkness was comforting. The closet, in the small bedroom, was her rabbit hole. Where she was hiding, she couldn't see me, but she knew I was close. She didn't trust me and wanted me to go away. She didn't care if I was dead or alive. I didn't blame her. I was human. Human was scary.

The dots weren't helping any. It was hard to enjoy them when the sweet soul in the next room was in a bad place mentally. I was in a weird place, knowing that my next move didn't make any sense. My left foot was dangling precariously off the mattress. I moved it quickly. The nameless thing that was staring at it, almost ate it. Irrational fears have power, similar to memories, that play repeatedly in your mind, clinging to you like the jaws of a bull snake. My lovely dog was haunted by real and monstrous things in the physical world, nothing ghostly. A shadow of someone approaching. The sound of a door shutting. Keys jangling. The snap of a lock opening. They didn't issue a threat in my home, but they were alive and sneering at her inside her head, telling her that she was hopeless, a fool to believe that she was safe. I swore to the ceiling that I would smother her memories with enchantment, as much as possible.

I whispered a promise. She heard me. "I will make it better. I won't give up on you. You will claim your power, the magic of your soul, and the joy of being loved. You are beautiful, and you will feel it."

The dots must have agreed. They sparkled like fireflies. Seconds later, a gentle wash of white light flowed through me. It felt warm and delicious and inspiring, like hot chocolate chip cookies. I felt incredibly hopeful. There was more to it. It left me with a reminder. It wasn't about me or the gas bill or my hair color that wasn't working. It was all about love and taking care of each other - humans and animals and the wildflowers growing in my yard, excusing my dry dirt, begging for a spray of water.

For the next few months, the ordinary sounds of the evening, the hum of the heater or the ice machine gurgling, were overpowered by strange and unsettling noises, deep into the night. Shaula Pearl was a nocturnal creature, coming out of her closet on silent paws, poking around the house, as long as I was in bed staring at dots. Thump was becoming normal. It was her body slamming into the closet when something scared her. It didn't take much of anything. Even on vibrate, my cell phone was alarming and so was a plastic bag crinkling into a kitchen drawer. Also, crash was a common wake up call. She didn't have any spatial awareness, the same as a toddler who is aware of the chair but runs into it, lacking a sense of his body and where it is. She bumped into things often, instead of walking around them. It wasn't her eyesight. Later on, when she was less stressed, she could maneuver without damage. For the moment, what I worried about most was her head. In the first few months, she would jerk brutally or bolt so quickly from a noise or an unfamiliar object, her head would smack into a wall or a door frame. I could hear it in the kitchen, even if she was upstairs.

Night was now an adventure into the realms of the unknown. After the lights went out, possibilities seemed endless. Near the end of the third month, I heard a crash and then a long unsettling screech, making my toes curl. A loud whack, after that, threw me out of bed. There was no evidence of a whack in the living room, leaving only the kitchen. It was easy to locate at that point. My toaster was dead and buried under a paper bag and a dish towel. I had choices. I took the enchanted one. "Hey. It's okay," I said, as lighthearted as I could, believing that she could sense my emotions beyond verbal confession. "It only toasted on one side anyways. You did me a favor." By the time I was back in bed, I realized that it didn't really matter what was buried because it wasn't her. You shift priorities when you focus on love and healing. A toaster held an important position in my kitchen. I love toast. I can't live with toast. On the other hand, there was no place on earth, I could replace Shaula Pearl.

The classic bumps in the night, the hair raising prickles, were now a part of my life, but it was only the bare beginnings of our extraordinary journey together. She wrote it, and I typed it, exactly as it happened, and if parts of it are hard to believe, trust her. Animals have no words in their language for deception.

Divine Light connected me to a very sweet and gentle soul. I couldn't be anything but honest, or it wouldn't work. Truth is standing under the stars, dropping your ego, revealing everything of importance. It involves a disrobing, in a sense, exposing the real you, and after that, yelling your name, claiming who you are, what you believe in. Hunger for the passion and longings of your own life, the pursuit of your own journey without apologizing. A dog taught me that.

Shaula Pearl has revamped and enchanted my own life for the past five years. She looks older now with a soft interlace of gray, circling the pink spot on her nose, and little threads of white sprouting around her eyes. Her eyebrows are charming arcs of silver flecked with black. She doesn't get on the bed as much, and it's hard for her to get up and down off the floor, but her eyes sparkle and her paws prance.

Her most recent birthday party was celebrated in true Shaula Pearl fashion. Light bulbs and the TV were not invited, since they make her nervous, and my phone was banned in the bathroom with the door shut. I turned on music designed for relaxing the dog brain and then lit candles. I offered her an enchanted biscuit smeared with peanut butter and a full body massage with lavender oil. After that, I worked on some book ideas with one ear listening, as usual. A few minutes later, I heard a bark, clipped and to the point. I pried my fingers off the keyboard and investigated. Her favorite toy, the brown paper bag, was ripped apart, covering the living room carpet. I smiled, pushing a large, damp piece of it away from her red ball, in case she couldn't find it. "Good shred," I said, picking up the obvious pieces, moving as quietly as I could. Even now, she likes me to move slow and composed and to control my emotional state. If I shriek with joy, she bolts to her sacred space, her closet. At least the hard thump is gone. She runs in it with more grace.

For Shaula Pearl, enchantment was not an option. Her needs were on fire, raging at a highly volatile level, threatening her life. Anything less potent would have been non-effective. Now, she wags her tail, woofs her opinion and drools over toast. She explodes with joy during one her thunderous gallops around the house. It's a divine sensation, every soul has the right to experience, whether it's loving yourself, loving someone else, or loving the fact that you are alive, and you can dance in a silver robe under an awning of stars if it makes you happy.

Driving home from the animal shelter, with Shaula Pearl in the back seat, gave me little indication of the magic to come. She was stiff and staring wildly at everything, like a zombie dog, but she wasn't in a full blown panic. I spoke to her many times, telling her that I loved her, knowing that she didn't understand. Trust was critical and that was about as far away as the moon. I had supporters. Winnie-the-Pooh walked in, eating out of his honey pot. He lives in my head, being one of his most ardent fans. His words, always unpretentious and with their own brand of enchantment, gave me hope. "I had traveled out of my own safe place in the forest, to venture out and meet those I am supposed to meet." He applauded my effort, even if no one else did. Also, he would have said, "If the person you are talking to, doesn't appear to be listening, be patient. It may simply be that he has a small piece of fluff in his ear." I am sure she did, and the fluff was deadly. It was the residue of abuse.

Before Shaula Pearl, I was Mesa and Wicca's human. Mesa was a brown lab, dark and lusciously chocolate. She was one big, sweet truffle. If I walked her at night, strangers would argue with me that she was a black lab and that I should know my dog. My answer was direct. "I know the difference between a milk chocolate butter cream and a dark Bordeaux, but thank you anyways." Wicca, on the other hand, was a mix of border collie and wonderful, in shades of yellow and gold, and sometimes an orangey red, depending on how the sun hit her. Now, they live in the spirit world, jubilantly alive and healthy, and very often, here at the house with me, playing with Shaula Pearl. They both relish the quiet hours of the night, strolling into my dreams with their goddess attitudes and bewitching grins.

Soon after Wicca passed, there she was, nudging me in a dream, staring at me saying, "What? I'm alive. You knew that." Her eyes gave her away, gleaming with a hint of mystery and amusement like they always did. Her strawberry blond hair was sparkling in the warmth of a perfect dream day, along with a new hairdo - rows of neon pink dread locks attached to her sides. "Nice," I said, nodding my head. Dog salons in the spirit world. Of course. Why not?" She grinned at me with her little pointy teeth, bouncing along with me instead of running a race, more her style.

I looked up at a towering magnolia tree, much like the one in my front yard, wondering if I was dreaming or if life was lapping into my dream. Maybe I was in both worlds. Wicca vanished for a moment, reappearing seconds later, her jaw quivering. She was murmuring something, so I leaned closer, hoping to hear what she was saying. I closed my eyes, opening them a moment later, frustrated and annoyed at my inability to stay asleep during significant moments. I begged the dream angels to reveal her message, fighting the urge to over-analyze it, knowing that I had a habit of finding symbols in just about anything, including marshmallows in hot chocolate. Nothing came in, so the best course of action was to count my feet and go back to sleep.

I was stopped cold. Two words, quietly spoken, changed the course of my life. "Get ready." I was more bewildered than frightened. The spirit world had thrown out a welcome mat, at the foot of my bed, when I was eight. Large groups of people, wearing beautiful robes, would enter my room through one wall and exit through another wall, going somewhere together, seemingly unaware of the young girl clutching her pink Easter bunny, waving at them.

So without hesitating, I answered the mysterious voice. "For what? A trip? A gift? Romance over a stem of broccoli at the market? Maybe I should eat better. I didn't get a yes from the universe, so I put in a request. It never hurts. An edible flower arrangement sprayed with dark chocolate. I waited. The universe was shaking its head, rolling its eyes. "Okay. I'm open," I said, already knowing that I would hear about it when it happened. I didn't have long to wait. Within the month, the impact of those two words revealed themselves. I had severely under-rated their meaning. Her name was Shaula Pearl.

Sometimes, you can see a journey off in the distance and do the ground work. When it arrives, everything falls into place. Flowers grow at your feet. The sun shines eternally in your lap. On the other hand, a journey can take you by surprise, a summer rainstorm bursting wildly, and you dash for cover, not sure where you're headed. There are no signs, stacked in the woods, with helpful warnings. Don't back up without extreme soul damage. High levels of anxiety ahead for at least three months. Without a doubt, the journey with Shaula Pearl was the storm, but it was an intentional excursion into the wild woods. I asked for it. I grabbed the adoption papers. I had questions. How can I help her? When can I take her home? What can I expect? Everyone at the shelter offered exceptional support and sent me home to do some prep work. The details of the pending journey were unknown. No one could tell me those. Perhaps it was a good thing. Knowing everything at once would be frightening.

I have a bad habit of assuming. This time, it gave me strength. I assumed that everything would be okay. I embraced the unfamiliar elements of my new journey because I didn't really know what I had done. My heart had taken the lead, stuffing my head into a lock box. Logic took a hike. At the same time, I was led by spirit, where logic is often hidden. I adopted a special needs rescue dog, age six, part border collie and part beautiful, with large black ears and a massive neck. Her dignity and self-worth had been stripped to the bone. The hoarder left nothing, almost. She was still breathing and eating, barely. She was alive in the physical sense, but she was emotionally dying, fearful to be alive.

Five years later, I understand and appreciate what it means to enchant, although it's up for debate. Concern over the state of your carpet, is a normal reaction, easily outweighing an adoption fee. Your feet deserve creature comfort and two inch padding with compelling fragrances. It came down to options. I chose to save a soul, and somewhere along the way, she saved me from my less enchanted self. I dream more, and I hope more. The ordinary feels magical. Looking out of my window, as the sun slips discreetly below the horizon, ushering in the night sky, melting the shapes of trees and buildings, I hunger for more. But not in the material sense - more for the treasures of the soul, the inner wealth of myself.

At the same time, it hurts to remember our first official day together. It wasn't your typical doggie moment oozing with affection. Nobody heard a, "Hey girl. I'll pat my thigh and you trot over, the second half of your body on guarded jiggle." Instead, it was more like a horror movie without a script. She was staring at me in the middle of my living room. I was staring at her, wondering if she wanted to eat something. Me. It wasn't such a far-fetched idea. Her ribs were showing and mine weren't. Besides, the sides of her body were puffing in and out, a sure sign of anxiety.

What happened the next few minutes, made me realize how terrified Shaula Pearl truly was. She was pushing herself backwards, straining with such force, her cheeks were puffing out. Her head was at an odd angle, and a weird chirping sound was coming out of her mouth. I had a hard time holding onto her leash because my hand was sweating. I had never witnessed this kind of crushing fear in an animal. It was painful to watch, and it was done by a human. I felt guilty by association. In all honesty, I did have a moment of relapse, wondering what had truly compelled me to adopt a dog who was so different from Mesa or Wicca. I mentally slapped myself, knowing that I already loved her and that something beyond the realms of the earth bound had arranged it. The stars were in alignment. Spirit had spoken. We had found each other and that was that.

I told my worst enemy, the high ranking demon of doubt, to take a hike. Even so, I could hear him laughing at my delusions of enchantment. I focused on her face. Her eyes were shimmering with fear. Her large ears were not much better, plastered flat against the top of her head, almost invisible. Her tail was gone, tucked under her belly as far as it would go without snapping off. I felt helpless. She felt terrified.

There was no time to plot out a plan, and I couldn't remember anyone at the shelter mentioning the weird sound position. I shouldn't have worried. She took the lead, changing maneuvers. All straining stopped, all of a sudden. There was an odd feel to the moment, as though we were trapped in a snow globe, with time grinding to a dead stop. I didn't know what to do, so I smiled at her. I sent her love thoughts. I sat down on the carpet, hoping to look more like a big bunny, anything other than human. I didn't move. She didn't move. I had other pressing concerns. My bladder was having an opinion and so were my legs. Cramping could take this to a whole new level. If I stood up, I could lose my balance, pass out and wake up with a good view of her back molars.

My imagination was on over kill, as usual. I went over my options. She could live where she was standing. I could stake a sign in the carpet with an arrow pointing at her saying, "Dog lives - Here." I could force the issue. Bad enchantment karma. She could lunge at me, swallowing me in a few massive bites, and looking at the width of her neck, I would go down easily. "Pick one," I said, staring at my feet, wondering if I had already messed everything up. Eye contact was a threat of aggression in certain time warps. This would be one of them.

Within seconds, she began to hum deep in her throat. I had no idea what it meant, but it sounded like the next tone down would be a growl. Amazingly, concern over both of our mental states took a back seat. Her eyes gave me a message. They said, "Help. I'm in a really bad place." I could feel myself tearing up. There wasn't time. My cell phone intervened and not in a pleasant way. The room exploded.

My dog, yet to be enchanted, pulled the leash out of my fist, froze for a moment, jerked noticeably, and began racing around the small downstairs of my townhouse like a blind dust devil. I panicked, noticing a window open and the screen loose, and she was eyeing it. I could see her airborne, propelling herself through the window and hitting her head on the palm tree, a few feet away. Dog angels must have flown in at mock speed. She stalled in mid-air, dropping to the ground, panting. I grabbed the end of the leash, panting myself. "It's okay. You're safe," I told her, hoping against odds that she understood me. She responded in a way that I didn't expect. She sneezed. I wanted to cry, it was so normal. After that, a small sigh escaped her mouth, one of many to come.

Journeys are known for having a starting point and an ending, but it's a grand illusion. When something ends, a millisecond later, something begins. Life churns around and around like a giant wheel. The cycle is never-ending. The dark moon feasts upon the sun, flowering into a full moon. A sunset crushes colors together, pushing them into the night sky and reviving them at dawn. Shaula Pearl moved from a dark place to an enlightened closet. Her lumbering gait ended, and she prances now.

My dreams for her began at the animal shelter, five years ago, but the roots of our journey took hold over twenty years ago. My husband, at the time, gave me a birthday card with a short note. Go find your dog. It was better than a Gucci crocodile shoulder bag. A dog was a living soul, always a plus. I have two wonderful daughters, but they don't require a walk around the block twice a day, and they wouldn't appreciate belly rubs or squeaky toys resembling oversized hotdogs. In spite of my initial excitement, I went over my options. I considered the easy route. I imagined, No dog. No stressing over vacations if we couldn't take her. No exercise guilt if I decided to bake cookies because it was raining. Also, there was the hair issue on everything and the extra chores. Dog food. Washing dog beds. Checking ear canals for wax build up. Then I imagined, Yes dog. I saw someone who was looking at me as if I was the most wonderful soul in the whole world, without makeup. The yes won.

The connecting threads of our souls, gossamer in appearance but strong as silk, weave us together in a vast, cosmic web, from soft blankets of grass to the far-flung stars. We live in this divine matrix of light, sifting through everything - dew drops and red maple leaves and ice crystals in clouds. Our thoughts, as transient as they might be, and the smallest of our actions, stream outward, blending with all souls, and like charcoal sketches, they shade our lives. We fill them in. We lace together. Humans connecting to humans or to the souls of animals. Animals connecting with each other, in ways that are far from obvious. Mesa linked to Wicca and Wicca to Shaula Pearl, in one of the most selfless ways possible. It involved Wicca's death.

With that said, Mesa and Wicca were exceptional souls with their own journeys, knee deep in the extraordinary and worth sharing. The spiritual side of them manifested at a fast pace. By the time Shaula Pearl arrived, the veil between the two worlds, the physical and the spiritual, ripped wide open. My own innate sensitivity to the spiritual realms, increased almost overnight in leaps and bounds. I saw colors I hadn't seen before, making the world rich in detail. I heard choirs of angels and heavenly music when my radio was off. Love became everything without physical boundaries and conditions. Love holds the universe together. It holds Shaula Pearl together. Without it, there would be nothing - no joy, no enchantment, no hope for a soul that didn't believe in being alive.

Besides the amazing and restorative power of love, joy became more than an emotion. It became something alive and solid, blasting out of Shaula Pearl, her soul on fire. Her joy run is priceless and incomparable to anything I have ever seen. Joy is dog. Joy is human. We both feel it, sharing the same brain structures and dealing with similar emotions and distinct personalities. What seems odd to be me, is the time spent on comparing animals to humans, wanting to prove things, to stress the point that we are more highly evolved, more multifaceted in our thinking. Why do we do this? Why is it so important? We are all different but equal in our differences.

To some people, Shaula Pearl is only a dog in a closet, labeled sad dog, boring dog, sweet but not too smart of a dog. She is none of the above. She is right up there with the human race. She has emotions and preferences and intelligence. In all fairness, I know humans who are magnificently caring and affectionate. I know humans who are less dependable and trustworthy than animals. I've seen dogs with flashes of brilliant creativity. I've seen humans with no flashes. Just live. Thrive with mammoth amounts of passion, spilling over into your cookie dough, into your peppermint mocha. Indulge. Grin. Take notes. Embrace yourself. Love others. Believe in the divinity of your own soul and the soul of everyone else's.

Shaula Pearl's journey encompasses so many facets of a lifetime. It hurts. It aches. It throbs with fear. At the same time, during moments of exquisite beauty, it glows in the night and sparkles during the day, rousing her spirit, telling her that she's worth everything, that her soul matters. It is also one of the most profound experiences I have ever had, changing the way I breathe and move, the way I think and the way I love.

I'm not the only one who seems enchanted by her. Friends who visit my joy-ravaged home, sense something special about her. They look in her eyes, and they feel things – the deepness of life and the mysteries of it, awakening hidden emotions. They see things at my house, making them ponder upon the existence of other worlds. Twila, a good friend of mine, stopped in for a visit, the day after I brought Shaula Pearl home. I was told at the shelter that I should avoid visitors for at least a week, until she adapted to her new surroundings. I talked to her at the door, explaining the situation. As Twila got in her car, she asked me if Shaula Pearl was enjoying the view. I didn't understand at first. She pointed to the bedroom window over the garage. There she was, with her white face and her large black nose. I ran into the house, thinking that she had escaped her crate and was running around in a full blown panic attack, ending up on the top of my desk. I was relieved to find her sitting in her crate with her eyes half closed.

Shaula Pearl's face has been on my window ever since I brought her home. You can't wash it off, and you can't see it from inside my bedroom. It is a manifestation of her spirit guarding the house.

CHAPTER TWO

SACRED CHOCOLATE

*It's not what you look at that
matters, it's what you see"
Henry David Thoreau*

Mesa, my dark chocolate lab, helped me to understand, more than I ever had, that dogs have a spiritual side. She nudged me into it, most likely knowing that Wicca was coming and that she would hurl me into it. As a result, it's fair to say, that Mesa introduced me to the sacred membership of the dog hood. My parents encouraged it, years before I was handed the key or the pooper scooper. They were life-long members, cultivating my thirst for animal companionship. Dad came home from work and sat at his desk with his dogs wrapped around his feet. Didn't all dads? I thought mothers rescued birds. The cardinal would hang out in the freezer, on top of the frozen turkey. Wasn't that normal? My sister put up with lost iguanas, somewhere in the bedroom, because I couldn't find them. My brother and I shared a snake, a black indigo. I couldn't be the only teenager sneaking a snake into a mall.

The word 'own' rubs me the wrong way. I own my house and my car and my bag of chocolate chips. I owned the papers to Mesa but not her soul. I learned this from my parents - the joys of dog partnership, not ownership. The animals in our house shared our lives with us. They were respected and admired for who they were, including the sparrow we had for many years. My Mother attempted, numerous times, to release him into the wilds of our backyard. Every time she did, he flew to our screen door, clutching it.

As a result of my upbringing, I searched for my dream dog with serious intent, knowing that animal personalities are as varied as humans. A good match was important. A friend rallied me on, complaining at the same time. Her new puppy, a Chihuahua and rat terrier mix, was so feisty, she didn't have the energy to keep up with him. I told her to commit and grin. She wished me luck, looking a bit haggard. Her dog was nipping her heels, pulling on her socks, and growling, all at the same time - a little joy party.

The hunt was on. I was sure about one thing, founded on my own penchant for dark chocolate butter creams. I wanted a brown lab. I was sure about two things, more on an esoteric level. She was out there waiting for me, wondering why it was taking me so long to find her, and she was female. I had a feeling we had met before, friends on the other side, with me, scratching her spiritual ear, plotting our journey together. I didn't tell many people that I could sense things. My mother was aware of it. Growing up, she had similar experiences with the spirit world, many of them in her own bedroom. Nocturnal travelers, sifting through walls, could be a genetic trait. But it gave me hope that I wasn't crazy and that life was full of dog magic and mysterious murmurings, all from a divine source.

I was brimming with optimism that I would fly to my dream dog, with the velvety whispers of angels guiding my spiritual compass. Wearing my lucky jeans, which was pretty much every pair, plus my favorite t-shirt to buoy my hopes, I visited many homes, presenting their puppies in full gala mode - girls with pink bows in their hair and blankets on the floor covered with large dog heads. I felt appreciated and a little nuts, sitting with a gooey smile on my face, trying to maintain an appearance of normalcy. I was positive, that within a week, she would materialize out of the squirming masses, and I would know, in a flood of divine inspiration, who she was. Any preconceived notion of how it would happen, flushed down the drain. I felt nothing. I thought I was doing it the right way. I was confident in my request, asking the universe for the preassembled, ready to go puppy, yelping my name. Instant puppy gratification was on my prayer list. I didn't want to wait. I wanted her now.

"Hey. Anyone up there listening?" I asked, slumping in the seat of my car, driving home again, empty handed. "I'm doing my part. I'm searching. I'm saying positive affirmations. I will find her. I am finding her. I did find her." I said it differently a few times, in case I was saying it wrong, and spirit was being persnickety about it. Maybe it wasn't important enough. A momentous request. Earth-shattering. No. I knew better. You can request angelic assistance to find you a parking space, a lost cell phone or a twenty-four hour donut shop. My perfectly designed dog, a dark silky chocolate with a shimmer of mischief in her eyes, would manifest. This was dog serious. The pressure was on. I called my mother, requesting gut support. Her thick chicken and wild rice soup was magic and could mend anything, and if I sounded stressed enough, maybe she would throw in her orange cookies. Dad helped, too. The following morning, he gave me his newspaper. "Check the want-ads," he suggested, dunking a donut in his coffee.

I was hopeful. His simple and direct wisdom had a good track record with a good dunk. He was right, as usual. Between the hand-fed parrots and a baby chinchilla, were the enchanted words, "Labs for sale. Yellow, black and chocolate. Call for more information." I knew it. I could feel it, mixing in with the fruity scent of orange rind and brown sugar. Mother was baking. I called, trying to sound excited but sane. Interested without panic. I must have pulled it off. I was cordially invited to see the puppies within the hour.

I was met by a tall lady in dusty jeans. Her smile didn't seem right. It was stretched more than it should be, mirroring the grin of a jack-o-lantern. Nerve attack on my part. I smiled back, sure that mine was all lopsided, and my eyes, way too eager, making me look like a mad, obsessed seeker of the golden puppy. I introduced myself, as likable as I could, agreeing with everything she said. It must have worked. She invited me into the inner sanctuary, the holy ground in my head, where the puppies lived, instructing me to sit on the dirt and wait. Within seconds, puppies assaulted me from all directions, in all three colors, tumbling over each other, trying to reach the human. They were eight to ten weeks old, chubby and soft as silk, with a few runts scrambling to keep up. I was having way too much fun. My hair tie was slipping.

The tall lady didn't say much. She excused herself shortly after, disappearing into a small office building, close by. Five minutes later, I stood up brushing off puppies. My hands were empty, again. My dog wasn't there. I didn't get it. I was frustrated beyond words, telling myself that something was seriously wrong with me. I took a few defeated steps toward the office, looking over my shoulder, to wish them all a beautiful life, and there she was.

She was sitting on her hind legs, regal looking and staring at me as if she knew exactly who I was. She was older than the other puppies, by at least two months. My puppy is younger, but fate was staring me in the eyes, telling me I was wrong. I was stubborn. No. My puppy is tiny, snuggling in my hands, kissing my neck with her little wisp of a tongue. I know what I wanted. It didn't matter. Divine Light was not in the mood for conflict. I was told without compromise - "This is the dog you are supposed to be with. It's a contract thing." I nodded, open to being wrong, knowing that my dream dog was at stake. I approached her slowly, dropping to my knees, rubbing the hair under her chin. Eye level now, something passed between us. It was silent and golden. The heart had spoken. We had found each other.

Check list. Humans can be stubborn. Brown. Yes, she was dark brown, except for a small patch of white on her chest. I could handle a smear of white chocolate. Female. I didn't check. I just figured. Sweet. She was already staring at me with those dog eyes. Smart. She knew. When it came to her age, I gave in. I should never assume that I have it right. Divine light is aware of my path and has no qualms about guiding me. Her tail took off, thumping the dirt, agreeing with me. I spoke quietly to my accomplice. "Wait until we get in the car. After that, we can have a chocolate meltdown. We still have to get past the tall lady and the gate."

She knew what I said. She was watching me intently, her eyes dancing with mischief. "I'll be right back," I whispered. "Wait here. You're going home with me." My thumb was twitching and my heart thumping, walking up a short flight of stairs, ending at the tall ladies office. I was ready for a fight, if necessary. Maybe she wasn't for sale? If that was the case, I would beg. Roll over. Promise her orange cookies.

The tall lady looked at me, shuffling some papers, acting like she was fake busy. It was nerves again, playing tricks on me. I went with it. She spied on people in the dirt, wanting to make sure they didn't have any saliva phobias or allergies to affection. "Pull it together," I thought, clearing my throat, acting as nonchalant as I could. "I found her," was all I said, trying to be cool but not cold. I was making it harder than it was.

"Which one?" she asked me, with a letter opening in her hand. My thoughts were all over the place. If I gave the wrong answer, she could be dangerous.

"That one." I said, pointing to my dream dog, who was still sitting in the same position, eyeing me like I was a nut case.

"The older one? The dark chocolate one?" she asked, fiddling with the letter opener.

"Yes! Who do you think it is. She's the only one staring at me!" I didn't say that. I did say, "Yes. That's the one. She's beautiful."

"Okay. I have a few questions to ask you," she said, putting the letter opener down and picking up a pencil, twiddling it between her first finger and her thumb. Nerves make me observant.

She interviewed me in full twiddle. "Do you have a secure yard? Where will she sleep? Who else do you live with? Do you have other dogs? Why do you want a chocolate lab? It's a popular color."

That was the question that worried me, sensing the importance of it. "I'm not sure," I said, being honest. "I love the color brown. She's the one I've been looking for. We bonded." I didn't tell her that I was divinely guided, a glaze donut solidified the deal, and that I loved to eat dark chocolate.

Three hundred dollars passed between us, and she was mine. I was hers, to be fair. I drove off with my dream dog in the back seat and avoiding the rear view mirror, afraid of the illogical - the tall lady running after me, demanding that I stop, that I wasn't the right person to have an enchanted supply of dark chocolate, in the shape of a dog, for at least twelve years. Not being one to tempt fate, I looked over my shoulder instead. My dream dog made kind of a huffy sound and relaxed, putting her head on her paws. She didn't move after that, until I arrived at my parent's home. She barked once, as I parked the car. It was more of a statement. It was final. The deal done. Contract no longer pending. I goose-bumped.

A.A. Milne, the creator of the Pooh Bear, had it pegged. "I knew when I met you, an adventure was going to happen."

Mesa had the run of the house, but she loved the backyard. It was full of rabbits. She participated in many of their uninhibited and joyful activities. Often, she would look through the glass doors, tell me that she was rabbit queen, and off she would go, running and jumping all over the yard, playing with them.

They adopted her into their family, pretending she was a giant brown bunny. Their obvious affection extended to the realms of the physical, something Mesa put up with, but I don't believe ever fully consummated. I never saw any dark chocolate lab-a-rabbits hopping around with large brown noses. Mama and Papa rabbit were just very affectionate, anywhere, but they enjoyed the privacy of their large hutch. It was more of a love shack where they snuggled together, creating babies at least twice a year. I gave them away to good homes that had no intentions of putting them in small enclosed cages, crunching up their powerful hind legs. One Easter morning, my two daughters and I saw eight baby bunnies decorating the grass. If there was ever a message of rebirth, this was it.

No matter the amount of fluffy abundance, Mesa never tired of them, spending hours in the backyard, romping around with their wild, primal energy. Mama rabbit was fickle, smitten with the brown creature, overlooking obvious differences. She did spins around Mesa often, her own version of a joy dance, jumping and twisting in mid-air. Mesa would watch her for few minutes, stretch, pretend that she wasn't impressed and then fly in, always cognizant of the fact that she was bigger and stronger.

My vet never fully believed the stories about them, assuming I was stretching the truth. In his head, dogs chased rabbits and ate them. Not Mesa. She never went after them in an aggressive manner, but she did retrieve the babies who would pass away, too weak to survive more than a few days. Gently, she would carry a limp bunny in her mouth, dropping it at my feet, no matter where I was in the house. She would sit patiently, waiting for me to bury it, which was pretty quickly.

One afternoon, I was pulling some weeds, admiring their willfulness to colonize the backyard. I flattered them often, trying to get on their good side, pushing the idea of how deserving they were of a more elegant yard. They never took me seriously, always coming back taller and thicker. In truth, I did like their bright, yellow flowers, coloring my otherwise drab lawn, but on this particular day, nothing looked inspiring. I felt dog-tired, yanking them up with weak apologizes for curbing their life span. The sun was in full harvest mode, nourishing my wide variety of wild plants, but it was depleting my strength. I sought the kitchen for a chocolate power drink. When I returned to the yard, I couldn't see Mesa or the rabbits. It didn't make sense. I looked in the only place I could think of - the large igloo shaped doghouse on the patio. I expected to see at Mesa, all curled up with her paws crossed. What I did see, made me a believer in the depth of animal relationships. Mama bunny was in the igloo with her latest litter.

She thumped her hind leg, telling me to control myself and not get all emotional over it. I could frighten her babies. "Okay," I said, sensing her own intuitiveness about me. "It's roomier. It's more private. You want a new bedroom. I get that, but where's Mesa?" I glanced around the yard, baffled. A moment later, I saw her. She was in the love shack, curled up in a tight ball with her eyes closed. Mesa was a gracious soul, taking the only room available. Dog in rabbit cage. Nope. My vet would never believe this one.

Mesa did many amazing things, but one thing she did, out ranked the love shack but not by much. My oldest daughter Rachael, was dating somebody that Mesa wasn't particularly fond of. I didn't blame her, in this case. He never acknowledged her presence. There might have been more to it. Dogs have a third eye packed in fur, in the middle of their forehead, seeing things that we aren't always aware of.

One night in particular, made me a believer. It was raining hard with an icy wind, dropping the temperature below sixty, which for Ventura, is complain weather. There was a loud knock at the door. Mesa flew off the couch, barking. It made me nervous. Most of the time, she was quiet when someone showed up. I looked through the peephole, seeing the guy on Mesa's ignore list, standing on the porch with his head down. I invited him in, explaining that Rachael was still at work and would be for a few more hours. He didn't look very good, so I asked him if he was feeling okay. He said no, asking me if he could lie down for a few minutes. I said yes, leading him to the small upstairs bedroom.

When he left an hour later, Mesa trotted upstairs. I wondered what she was up to. She rarely went anywhere in the house without me. She came down soon after, jumping on the couch, ignoring me. I knew my dog. Something was up. It didn't take long to figure it out. A peculiar odor, odd for the house, led me to the top of the stairs. Mesa had left something large and brown on the bed that he had slept on. She voiced her opinion.

Mama and Papa rabbit were ten years old when they passed away. Surprisingly, their last litter was not in the love shack or the igloo. It was behind the piano in my dining room, and I have no idea how that happened. For the first time, I kept a bunny, mainly because he never wanted to go outside. If we put him in the yard, he would sit by the glass doors, staring into the dining room, his little head, darting back and forth like a squirrel. He was looking for Mesa. He was always following her around, inside or outside. He was dog enchanted.

We named him Uno, because he was one amazing bunny. Bedtime was interesting. I would go up the stairs, followed by Mesa and Uno.

I would get in bed, followed by Mesa and Uno. In the middle of the night, Uno would either be sprawled across my back, or Mesa's back. If I moved him, he would hop around the bed and curl up in a big ball of fluff by Mesa's neck. It seemed normal at the time.

Mesa was one amazing dog. She began to show serious signs of aging when she was thirteen. One month, shy of fourteen years, she couldn't walk up the stairs and would howl at night when I went to bed. You commit when your dog is old. I made her a bed in the kitchen and would sit by her for a while, eventually pretending that I was sleeping. When she closed her eyes, dropping her head, I would sneak upstairs. Often, she would wake up in the middle of the night and howl again.

My vet gave me kindly warnings that year, that she was bypassing the average life span for a lab. He thought it was all the good food and care she received. I didn't tell him about the pound of dark chocolate she found under the Christmas tree one year, leaving me one almond cup, and I didn't tell him about the chocolate chips when I was baking. I believed his advice. The killer is the caffeine and the size of your dog. Regardless of what you do, the heart has a shelf life and a retirement plan. One night, she stopped eating and drinking. I slept in the living room with her, gently petting her and telling her how wonderful she was and how much she meant to me. I called my vet in the morning, cringing at his words. Within twenty-four hours, if she didn't pass on her own, I needed to euthanize her.

That was not happening. I told Mesa that her home was the best place to pass over. It was where she grew up, where she loved the rabbits, where she ate chocolate. Mesa was old, but she was not in pain. She was walking around like a wise, old goddess, slow and deliberate, with her head bowed, full of dog wisdom. By the evening, she was noticeably uncomfortable. She would lie down, get up, walk around the room and lie down again, every five minutes. She came over to me once, bumping her head on arm. I broke down, turning my face. I didn't want her to see me cry.

Later that night, I put eye drops in her eyes to prevent dryness. I pushed a capsule down her throat to help calm her stomach. Close to midnight, she collapsed on her side. I sat by her, talking to her, telling her that it was okay to go, that it would be easy to pass over. All she had to do, was slip out of her beautiful, brown skin, and she would feel young and healthy again. She could eat spiritual chocolate. She could sleep with me, on top of me. I didn't care. She started to seizure, her legs quivering. I placed my hand on her side. As soon as I touched her, she was still. Finally, she didn't move at all. Her eyes shut, and her breathing slowed. I went upstairs for barely a minute. When I came back down, she was gone.

I held her close. I rocked her. I sobbed quietly. I was stunned at death, aware of his mission, the Lord of Shadows, gathering his souls. At the same time, when it happens, it doesn't feel real. It's too much of a change, life and death. It smacks you into the reality of it. I wiped my face and the back of her neck, dotted with tears. Jasmyne, my eight year old granddaughter, at the time, was upstairs sleeping. Death could wait on his announcement. I wrapped my dream dog in her favorite blanket, sitting by her the rest of the night. In the morning, I put her in the backseat of my car. Jasmyne wanted to go with us to the vet, choosing to sit with Mesa.

My vet's office was only ten minutes away. Somehow, I kept missing the street. Jasmyne was on to me. "Grandma," she said, quietly. "You need to take Mesa to the vet."

"In a few minutes," I told her, pulling into a drive-thru. "I really want a soda, bad. I promise, after that, we will go to the vet. Okay?"

"Sorry Mesa died, grandma," she said, her voice, shaky.

I looked in the rear view mirror, tears threatening. Jasmyne had Mesa's head on her lap. Old age had peppered her chocolate muzzle with silver. I looked at it, surprised. I knew she was graying, but I ignored it, day after day. Now, it was all I saw. "Age is a gift," I said, loud enough for Jasmyne to hear me. "She was here with us for a long time. She's still with us." Secretly, I was thinking, "Nope. There is no way that I'm leaving her body with the vet.

We pulled up behind his office, watching him wave us down. I lost it. The floodgates opened, pouring out of my eyes like a waterfall. All I could mutter was a drenched thank you, watching two assistants pull Mesa out of the backseat. Dead weight to them. How could they know? How could they grasp what she meant to me, to all of us, watching her lower jaw quiver when we hugged her, and kissing her chocolate ears, and every Christmas morning, watching her sit in the middle of the living room, on all the wrapping paper, and not budge an inch.

Almost forgetting, I reached into the glove compartment, pulled out a pair of scissors and shouted, "I need a part of her ear!" I said it all wrong, so I forgave the stares. I said it again. "I mean, I want a piece of her hair, close to her ear, where I kissed her all the time." Everyone nodded, reassured that I hadn't lost it. I looked at Jasmyne who was starting to cry. We hugged each other, watching Mesa vanish behind a cold white door. A pine box with her name on it would arrive within a week.

How do you say goodbye? You can't. It's impossible. It doesn't feel right. The finality of it is unreal, and it has nothing to do with your beliefs, as spiritual as they might be. Loss on the physical plane is traumatizing, even with animals. Not everyone understands dog loss. My brother Michael does. When he took his dog Wiley to the vet, for the last time, he felt such a deep and profound affection for his sweet dog. It was one of the hardest moments of his life. Love can render you speechless. The weight of words. Sometimes, there is no humanly way to express yourself.

The following evening, I was lying in bed, being stubborn, refusing to open my eyes. She wouldn't be on the bed, physically. At the same time, I knew better. She was there, I could sense her, but it wasn't enough. I wanted to know the precise location of her body. "Where are you?" I pleaded with her, patting the blanket. "I am not going to sleep, ever again, if you don't materialize, right now." I didn't sound very adult like. Mesa played into it. She licked my face with as much enthusiasm as she always did. For the next few months, she woke me often with her spectral kisses. Since then, I see her in my bedroom but not in her Mesa shape. Evidently, her charming ways are infinite, appearing to me as a churning swirl of dark chocolate chasing her tail.

The last time I saw her, she was swirling at the foot of my bed, a vortex of joy. The next day, wondering with my earthy brain, if I had truly seen her, I called my good friend Julia, who has marvelous psychic abilities. We swapped stories about weight gain, the meaning of life and blood pressure. Then we attacked the most traumatizing element of life - dating. After we shared horror stories, I was about to bring up Mesa, when Julia said to me, "You saw your dog, didn't you? A rock-solid confirmation from spirit, can harvest a crop of hope, lasting years. I would need it.

It's funny what your mind remembers. I was sitting in the lobby of my vet's office, with Mesa, barely a year old. There was a lady across from us with a dog who was sniffing my feet. I didn't mind, being a dog person. She apologized with great concern, as if her dog had bitten my toes off. I wanted to put her at ease, so I struck up a conversation. I asked her what kind of dog was so cordially exploring my scent. She smiled at her dog and answered, "His name is Zeus. He's a brown lab. Pure bred. Great lineage." Zeus was soulfully sweet, but he had giraffe legs and a head the size of a basketball. Not lab. Not important enough to explain it. She asked me the same question. I replied without any conceit. "She's a lab. Pure chocolate." It really didn't matter about the pure stuff. I was proud of her, because I loved her.

Mesa had been my best friend, my guide, my teacher. She didn't read books, but she had heart knowledge. She knew all about love. She was beautiful and caring and taught me about the amazing complexity of animals souls. Whatever powers there be, the dog must have been created from a celestial blueprint with high priority.

Mesa took care of me, my family, and the bunnies, and never asked for anything back but a good belly rub and carrots. Figures.

This world is full of magic and mystery. The flapping of a bird's wing, stirs my longing to fly. The iridescent shell of a beetle, under a maple leaf, shimmers in silent homage to its humble existence. Looking up at the night sky, I see the dreams of a divine mind, spiraling into the blackness of deep space, illuminating my journey. I stand in awe of the loveliness of unseen powers, supporting the diverse yearnings of my own singular reality.

The universe is well aware of what I need, what we all need. For me, it's family and the wild expression of nature, including dogs, chocolate and the realms of the supernatural. Mesa was on it. She came through to me, again, in a way that I would have never imagined in a million dog years. I was hosting my annual New Year's Eve party with all the trimmings, meaning a chocolate potluck. Toward the end of the evening, a surprise guest appeared in my camera. It was an orb, round and white, larger than a dinner plate. There was a delicate pattern in it, reminding me of a lace doily. Having read about them, there seems to be a debate - dust particles or spirit orbs. An orb in your camera could be either one. The orb that night, was spirit. I took some more pictures, one after the other. Each time, the orb moved a few feet to the right, traveling across a large wall by the front door. This orb appears in many of the photographs in this book. It is my mother's spiritual monogram.

A few nights after the party, I took a late night stroll in the backyard, walking the wood planks. I was missing Mesa. I wanted a sign from her, now. I had my camera with me and took a picture of the sky. Between my two palm trees, the guardians of my yard, was a large, shimmering heart-shaped orb. The heart is Mesa's monogram. My beautiful lab with the dark chocolate coat, oil-slick black at night, fooling the innocent, was out walking with me.

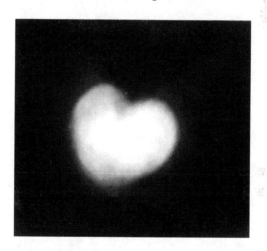

Pooh would say, "Think it over, think it under." Experiment and explore. Study what fuels your passion. From what I've witnessed, spirit can appear to you in any desired form, for it has no physical boundaries, fluid and ever-changing, like the wraithlike movements of a candle flame. It can fold into the space between leaves, shifting with the colors of dappled light. It can appear as an orb, a shadow, a defined shape, or a whirlpool of chocolate cotton candy in your bedroom.

CHAPTER THREE

DUST OFF YOUR WINGS

"A morning glory at my window,
satisfies me more
than the metaphysics of books."
Walt Whitman

Mesa was a queen of dogs. She was calm and dignified, unless she was rabbit dancing. Wicca was my second experience being a dog's human. She was only two when Mesa passed away, morphing instantly into queen hood. If Mesa was refined chocolate, Wicca was nuts and caramel, a scrumptious blend of wild energy, hurdling herself through life, an eternal spring of joy, defying the pull of gravity.

I found her in a local market, stuffed in a small cardboard box with three male siblings, all flea-ridden and free to the sucker who stuck her hand in and pulled one out. It was the easiest and most irrational magic trick, I ever attempted. I had never considered another dog besides Mesa. I would find her a home. I would. No, not mine. Somebody else's. Nope. Won't happen. Welcome home, Wicca.

I still think back on that illogical, split-second decision involving my hand, as innocent as it looks, cradling a puppy against my heart. But it was a fated act, directly connected to the survival of Shaula Pearl. As I drove home that day, with somebody else's puppy, grinning at me over the edge of a box, I had no idea of the magnitude of my decision. But I did know what was coming within minutes. There would be no doggie blessing on the new-comer from Mesa, the dark goddess who guarded our sacred grove, our home. There was no time for an apology. The cards had been dealt quickly. A force, more powerful than my own mortal doubts, was having its say.

Some of the most endearing and poignant moments of my life, which seem to be dog highlighted, were spinning my way. It was called Wicca. She wasn't a controlled whirl with royal attitude. She was lustful and wild. She was one of the most vibrant and joyous spirits I had ever met, and had only six more years to live.

I noticed a lump on her chest. It was small, about the size of an almond. The next day, it was noticeably larger. We went to the vet, figuring it was a wart, a beauty bump, a wad of joy tissue with no place to go. A few days later, I met with my doctor in a small room with glaring white lights and stainless steel instruments. He was playing slightly with his stethoscope. Nervous energy. Not good. "I'm sorry. It's cancer," he said, delicately. "It's a mast cell tumor, the most aggressive kind. Let's talk about options." My vet had no other way to say it. A rose is a rose, no matter how you look at it, no matter how hard you plead with it to be something else. He was smiling at me with a tight smile, a required smile. I nodded my head, blinking back tears. Pain was coming at me like a freight train without brakes.

My sweet and gracious vet had issued a death sentence, in his head. Mine was screaming, "No. This is not happening." What I really wanted to do, was yell into his stethoscope that he was wrong, that all his medical training was way off, and he was having a really bad diagnostic day. And options? What options? Wicca wasn't going to die, simple as that. I wouldn't believe it. I couldn't go there. I stood in his office, staring at him. He asked me if I was okay. I said, "Yes." I couldn't say much of anything else, knowing that my words would only clump out of my mouth, and I'd look like a fish gasping for air. I looked at Wicca, who was grinning at me and wagging her tail, her eyes dancing with joy, her stance on everything. It held true to her last breath.

After meeting with the doctor, heart shaped orbs began to appear in her photos. I showed them to her. She would look at them, stare at something in the room, and then fly off chasing it. The 'it' was Mesa, playing with her often but not for extended periods. Wicca's illness was making her weak and bone thin.

I never told Wicca that she was sick. I never said the word cancer in front of her. I called it Mr. C. Anyone who came over to the house, was not allowed to say the word or mention anything negative or depressing. That was a little tricky. A fair share of people, all with good intentions, would sneak in a "Poor baby. She's so thin." I would say, "She doesn't eat much." Others would say, "How much longer does she have?" I would say, "I don't know. I don't focus on it." The most painful comment was, "Are you going to put her to sleep?" My reply was, "I won't have to." I got some questionable stares with that one, but I stuck to it. I believed it. It seems immoral to pick the date and time of your pet's death. Passing over is sacred. Dogs should go the way nature intended. On the other hand, I admit that if your dog is suffering, it is a gift to hurry in death, or a nicer way to put it, to send your animal home.

Life is fragile, as wispy as the wings of dragonflies. Even so, we feel immortal, most of the time. A cut on our arm, heals within days. A sprained muscle gets better and better. The grim reaper can seem mythical, in your teens, when you feel that death is a thousand light years away. But he has a good side. He wants you to live, to do what makes you happy, to open doors that bring you pleasure and to close doors that hurt you. He wants you to grin, wag your tail, drool over something yummy, and embrace life with a hunger for nuts and caramel. Wicca taught me that. All I could do was hope that she would live, with her shameless amount of joy, for many more years. If I was wrong, she would die in a spark of happy, if I had anything to say about it.

Appointments were lined up. First, to see a specialist at a cancer clinic for dogs. We sat in a large, busy waiting area. I was trying to look positive and relaxed, smiling at the other dogs, but my insides were twisting. After about fifteen minutes, a young man entered the room with a clip board and yelled, "Wicca." She stood up, walking briskly over to him, wagging her tail. He asked me a question. "She knows her name?"

You can imagine my thoughts. "Do you know your name? Gee. I wonder why? Maybe because it's your name, and you've heard it a million times." To be rude is pointless, but I came close. Zero tolerance for dumb dog belief should be enforced.

Trying to be cordial, I said nothing. We followed him down a low lit hallway to a small room with almost all white accessories. It gave me the chills. I thanked the man without a name because I refused to remember it. The doctor arrived soon after, checking her out. He felt strongly about surgery, warning me at the same time, that a clean bill of health would be fifty-fifty. I agreed, feeling that it was the best option for the moment. I told Wicca how I felt about it. The doctor nodded. Wicca grinned.

The day of the surgery, I dropped her off at the Vet's office, telling her not to worry. Mommy wasn't worried. Mommy was happy that she would be feeling better. I drove to work, having no memory of how I arrived at my office. If people were late that day, I didn't notice, either. I couldn't swallow food, so I drank, tea, coffee, and soda. I had energy.

When I picked her up that evening, my vet looked pleased, explaining how confident he felt, concerning the removal of all cancer cells. He smiled, a nice un-tight smile, telling me that he had something highly unusual to show me. I followed him to a back room where all of the animals, who had surgery that day, were recuperating. All dogs were asleep or drowsy from medication, except Wicca. She was sitting up, waiting for me. My doctor was truly puzzled, wondering how she could be so alert. She didn't need any assistance either, getting from the cage to the car. She jumped in the front seat, as though nothing out of the ordinary had happened.

We drove home together, with me, doing all of the talking. I told her that I was proud of her, that she was strong and brave, and her joy was amazing. I told her that I loved her grin and that it was more precious to me than diamonds or an everlasting supply of chocolate. I didn't pet her, but I kept my hand on her chest, helping her balance. I don't think she wanted to admit it, but she was wobbly. Normally expressive, she was quiet, except for a little noise that she was making in her throat and coming out of her nose. I got teary-eyed, it was so her.

Things changed quickly, as she entered the house. Half way into the living room, her legs folded. She collapsed on the carpet, finally giving into the drugs. She intentionally waited. This took an amazing amount of willpower and love. Yes, she loved her home. I called Rachael to come over, wanting support. We sat by her, touching her lightly. She didn't move except for a little twitching of her eyes and her paws. No hint of a grin. The following morning, she was eating and drinking a little. By the afternoon, she was walking around the house, hunting for toys. Within a few days, she was dancing with her biscuits. One month later, Mr. C came back with a vengeance.

Mr. C was now on her right side and the size of a football. The cancer specialist gave me chemotherapy medication. The side effects were worse than the cancer. I called Julia. Wicca told her that she wanted to go naturally. She also expressed that she wanted to go to the beach, one more time, but knew it would be too strenuous for her. Before calling Julia, Wicca and I had talked about going to the beach. I threw the medication away.

Mr. C took her strength and her appetite, but he never took her passion for being alive. One memory in particular, haunts me. The night before she passed, she wanted to sleep with me, like she always did, but the heaviness of her tumor kept her on the floor. I made her a bed, almost identical to mine.

In the early hours of the morning, I sat up, hearing a soft, thumping sound. Wicca was at the foot of my bed, peering over the mattress, repeatedly. She was trying to jump up, but it seemed impossible. Her tumor was large and heavy, and she was weak. "Wicca. Don't jump up. It's okay," I said gently, but as firmly as I could. She proved me wrong. Her front paws hit the top of the bed, and one thump later, she was up. I stared at her in disbelief. She grinned at me and jumped down, falling into a deep sleep.

The next day, she stopped eating and drinking, but it didn't stop her tail. She wagged it constantly, a true testament to the power of joy. I talked to my Vet, knowing the outcome, the twenty-four warning. I gave her some medicine, helping her to relax. I played healing music. I told her what the Vet said and that it was time to ignore him. She needed to go on her own, just like Mesa. She wagged her tail, not concerned at all about the pending event. Dogs don't worry about death, like we do. It's a natural state. They accept it, and they don't argue with it, but they do worry about the people they're leaving.

That evening, we talked incessantly about many things – Mesa and the ocean and her favorite toy. We talked about my work and how it was a human thing to put value on a piece of paper called money. I told her that I needed it for the moment, until I could figure out how to grow dog biscuits in the garden. I also enlightened her on the merciless drone of work meetings or death by boredom. I was mandated to attend one, early in the morning, stressing the fact that Jasmyne would be at the house until I returned. I had only one request. If she was ready to pass over, she needed to let her know. At that point, I would come home, no matter what. We came to an agreement, after hashing over various options on how this might happen. She would go into the backyard and rest in the old doghouse, the one she had never used. After that, she would wait for me to get home. Before going to bed, I climbed into it myself, swiping out a bunch of cobwebs and leaves, wondering if I had gone loopy. Wicca came out to watch me. I took two pictures of her. In the first one, she's wearing a t-shirt covering her tumor. She's grinning at death, aware of the illusion.

The moon was not visible that night but a huge orb was. She sat motionless, staring at it. Somebody powerful and loving was helping. In the color photograph, the orb is a dark, rich amber color.

Later that night, I asked her a question, mentally. "What do you like to do? What makes you happy?" I have my own way of connecting - the Pearly Gate Method. It opens a gateway. Everyone has one. I laid in bed, thinking about how much I loved her. Then I imagined us sitting together, facing each other, a few feet apart. After a minute of breathing deeply, I visualized dots, glistening like small pearls, floating out of me like a spray of water, drifting towards her. At the same time, I imagined pearls, floating out of her, drifting towards me. Our pearls merged, flowing into each other. I waited, hoping to feel a connection. When that happened, I restated my question. After a minute, she said to me, "I like to play with my toys." It was the perfect answer. I had never seen a dog so joyously bond with her stuffed animals. She favored one in particular, a long stuffed dachshund, carrying it around with her at least half the day. I replaced it often.

One hour into my work day, Jasmyne called. All she said was, "Grandma. Wicca's in the old doghouse." I work a half an hour from home. The drive was a blur. The only thing I remember about it, are my words. I kept saying, "I'm coming sweet heart. Hold on. Mommy's coming."

I arrived home, making it into the backyard in less than five seconds. There she was, lying on her good side, half in and half out of the doghouse. The moment she knew I was there, she pushed herself out, her front paws digging in the dirt. She collapsed on the grass, seconds later. I sat by her, telling her stories of all the wonderful things we had done together, since she was puppy. I rubbed ice chips on her gums and her tongue, keeping them moist. I told her that it was okay to go, to unzip her fur. Slip out. Be light and free. She could fly on the bed, fly to the moon. Dance with orbs. Do whatever she felt like, grinning forever.

She looked at me in the eyes. I could read her. She was waiting for me to leave, like Mesa. Also, she was worried about me, going about my day without her. How soulful is that? I sat on the cement patio, five yards away, waving at her, trying to look like everything was fine, that I could enter my house without her banging into my legs, beating me in. Everything was a glorious game to her.

I didn't fool her. She left me a gift, knowing that I would need one. She lifted her head, looking up, wagging her tail. My mother was there, smiling at her. Then, she looked at me. Her eyes were gone, her physical eyes. In their place, were two faceted balls of light, the size of quarters. Her spiritual eyes were glowing with an unearthly radiance, I can't fully describe. What I was seeing, was not of this world. Her head fell on the grass, after that. She was gone.

She honored me, showing me a part of her soul. I felt it, also. It was sweet and shimmering with joy, and it had a vibrancy to it, warm and bright. Her energy was strong, and it was glowing like the sun, the moon and the stars, all coming undone together at the same time. It was everything she was. It was love energy.

"Piglet. How do you spell love? Pooh. You don't spell it. You feel it." A.A. Milne.

41

Sometimes, life unfolds in obscure ways. The feeling of fog. I can see it, rising out of the gray ocean, sea spray and salt crystals, the breath of an ancient sea monster, slithering up the small hill by my house, misty and damp, silent as the night sky. It travels a bewitching path, making me hunger for other worlds, where dreams and the lilac shadows of dusk, whisper to me, pulling me along, telling me where to go. I turned away, shutting the blinds, not wanting to listen. I was deaf in my loss. It didn't matter. Spirit was talking. Something was coming in. It was close.

I ignored the message, feeling numb. I was lonely for dog hair. I ate corn out of a can. I didn't care where my feet were, and I couldn't sleep. I was suffering from 'no-dog' insomnia. There were no lapping sounds at a water bowl. The dog toys, in the middle of the night, were silent. It was all wrong. Dog energy was missing. I felt ill. The emotional pain of losing Wicca, was very physical. My heart hurt.

Against all logic, I wanted another dog as soon as possible. I didn't know where to start. I mused over the idea that my dog knew. Maybe she was sitting at a corner, watching for Hondas painted grave yard rose, a wine colored base paint with mysterious layers of dust. She could be lounging at a cafe, sniffing people with a trace of dark chocolate on them. No matter what my hopes were, I was miserable. Friends told me to wait. Family wasn't sure what to tell me, knowing how much I loved Wicca and my insatiable need for paws.

Dreams. That was it, the simple solution as usual, as nontraditional as it might sound. Our thoughts and actions are governed by the constraints of logic, the rules of the conscious world, too often. I would dip into the lake of dreams with its watery colors of dark purples and midnight blues, swimming deep in the underground caverns of my soul, where I remember myself. It could work.

Lucid dreaming comes without effort, so I can't claim any mastery to the subject. When I was ten, the dream world laid out a welcome mat. I dreamed the same dream for years. I was awake in my dream, in a sense, knowing exactly who I was. I made the most of it, telling everyone in my dream what was about to happen. I have to admit, I was a dream brat. I never unveiled the ending. It's different now.

I'm conscious of who I am in my dreams, but I'm nicer. I talk to my dream people, telling them what I'm doing, what I'm writing about. They care because I make them care. Sometimes, characters that I'm writing about, appear in my dreams. I follow them around, taking mental notes on their conversations.

As a result of my journeys in the dream world, I went to bed, hopeful, saying positive affirmations. "I have found the dog who needs me. I am lying in bed with my dog. I see dog hair. I am joyful." The dots came in, shortly after, flashing more than usual. There was a large blue one to the right of my eye, up front and personal. "Whoever you are, help me," I pleaded, believing in the power of everything. If I gave this dot power, it would have it.

Close to sleep, I received a message, but it wasn't about my new dog. There was a well-defined thump at the end of the bed. Wicca was there, in the exact spot where she always landed, before she belly crawled up to my head, like I didn't know it. I didn't move, knowing it was a magical moment and how quickly they can vanish. Being human, I wanted more and more, another thump, a bark, a foot kiss, but Wicca had her own agenda. She shifted, getting comfortable. It must be a universal need in both realms.

I have an eclectic group of friends - college professors, preschool teachers, doctors, writers, shamans, energy healers and psychics. What keeps our friendships alive and vibrant, involves are feelings about life. We support the idea that all souls should be honored and that love and healing should be a worldwide cry. We see the heart and the soul of each other, nothing more. We each reflect the diversity of divine material. Our various spiritual paths, bind us together, not separate us. We understand that everyone has intellect and feelings, no matter who you are or what path you follow. A Buddhist or a Wiccan, has the same deepness of emotions for his family and his dog, as much as a Mormon or an agnostic. No one is less of a human. We all have our opinions about everything, and one passionately stated belief, doesn't necessarily work for anyone else. As plant eaters and meat eaters, we don't argue over who's right. We share our views peacefully over plates of asparagus and chicken legs.

With that said, I wasn't afraid to share. The thump story was a good one. I mentioned it to a few friends, readily agreeing with me that Wicca paid me a visit, except for one. She wondered if I had fallen asleep, and it was more of a dream thump. I told her that I was awake, simple as that. She asked me if I had ever dreamed that I was awake. This was going nowhere. At the same time, I understood what she was doing. She was trying to make sense of it all, in her own head, and examine it from all angles, having little experience with the spirit world. By the end of our conversation, she believed me, more than she didn't, but the idea of a ghost dog or even a loved one, appearing to her, was frightening. She couldn't explain why, but the confusion is obvious. We live in a physical word. We smell cinnamon sticks and wrap our hands around hot cups of coffee and bury our toes in warm, spongy sand. When we slip into the spiritual realms, off the GPS map, life becomes dreamlike, and very often, intimidating.

Julia is a big part of the thump story, no surprise there, considering that she pops into my life after odd experiences. I saw her the next day, ordering tea at a café, inside a local bookstore. I was standing in the same line, two people behind her. She turned around and her mouth dropped open. She grabbed her tea, bought me a hot chocolate and led me to the nearest table. Before I could say anything, she said a little too loudly, "You felt her! Your dog! She was in your bedroom!" I started to grin, noticing the expression on a lady who was sitting behind her. Julia wasn't finished. "Your dog really wants you to know that she was on your bed, that you didn't imagine it. Trust yourself with dogs!" I was trying not to laugh. I felt stunned at the same time. Connecting to spirit, feels so incredibly amazing, no matter how often it happens. At the same time, I can relate to my dear friend who was struggling with the idea that Wicca was still Wicca. The first time I saw a spirit, I screamed.

Our discussion that followed, turned a few heads. "Dogs are so much more than bones and hair. Can't people see that?" Julia was very exuberant, her voice, bellowing out over the crowd.

"Yes. Many people can," I said more controlled, hoping to calm her down, taking a long, slow sip of my drink, demonstrating constraint. That was hard for me. I then added, "Let's not forget paws." I almost lost it.

"In your wildest imagination, who else could it have been?" Julia asked, more in a conspirator fashion.

"My mother. She doesn't like me to worry about anything, but I can't imagine her thumping at the end of my bed, just to make me feel better." We hugged goodbye, promising to see each other soon, but figuring we would just run into each other.

The rest of the day turned into one of those do-nothing days. The Pooh Bear agreed. "Don't underestimate the value of doing nothing, of just going along, listening to all the things you can't hear." That's pretty much how it went. I walked my neighborhood, staying on the winding cement trails. A fair amount of dogs and their humans, were trying to keep pace with each other. Today, it seemed hauntingly depressing. I stared at my empty hands. No leash attached. No sniffing. No one crashing into bushes hoping to see something.

The second day without Wicca, all the bones in my body had headaches. I took aspirin. I laid in bed, begging for thumps. I ate a peanut butter sandwich, but it tasted like cardboard. I made brownies, hoping to increase my endorphins and feel better, but they tasted like chunks of dried mud. I couldn't find anything appealing. I ate more cardboard and mud, chasing it down with a soda, tasting like mouthwash. I was feeling stupid too, not able to keep a thought in my head, so thinking was out. I settled for the backyard, sitting on the wood planks, still feeling miserable. I felt guilty for feeling miserable. It wasn't about me. I was still breathing and not thinking.

There was nothing I needed to see, so I shut my eyes. I listened, unwillingly. The long palm fronds in my yard, dangling eye level, were swishing together from a slight breeze, creating wind chimes. The tree had become a leaf instrument, singing to me. Guilt again.

The world was so beautiful, but I didn't want it. I wanted stillness and darkness and black holes eating up everything. I felt a little dramatic, but it was my pain, and I could play with it however I wanted to. I also knew, that you have to embrace pain to release it. I listened again. A crow was cawing overhead, loud and persistent. He was sending me a message – crow, a symbol of transformation and change and the strength to push yourself beyond the limitations of this world. Also, the blackness of the crow, so beautiful, absorbing all the colors of the rainbow, all their energies, creating stability and balance.

Random enlightenment saved the moment. I felt better, reminding myself that the world held secrets to many mysteries. If we would eavesdrop more often, nature could be our teachers, streaming us memos daily. I closed my eyes, heeding my own advice, listening to the musical fronds, paying more attention, but my heart was numb. Numb was safe. It was then, I heard it - a faint bark, far away. At the same time, it was somewhere inside of me. I felt it, vibrating, bone-deep. It was crow's message. There was a dog who was in dire need of enchantment. The dog was a girl. She was starving, physically and emotionally. My numb heart would have to thaw itself out. I was needed somewhere else besides my pain.

CHAPTER FOUR

HEART KNOWLEDGE

The tree which moves some to tears
of joy, is in the eyes of others,
only a green thing that stands in the way."
William Blake

I admit, my imagination works tirelessly. I see images in tree bark. Rocks speak to me. The sky can be full of cloud dragons, miles long. As a result, a dog barking in my head, didn't seem that far-fetched. At the same time, I knew what I heard and felt, trusting my inner ear, the invisible ear that hears things beyond the vibrations of this world. The bark was real. Still, a part of me wanted a crawl space with insulation, a flashlight and a box of butterfingers. Hiding was numb.

Instead, I decided to write. Getting lost in words was always healing. I flowed into the realms of fantasy, of ghost rabbits and rainbow goblins. It helped, but I wanted to scratch an ear and drag stringy things out of eyes. I played the yes and no game. How would it feel to eat a piece of toast and not share it with anyone? Greedy? How would it feel to say goodnight to only yourself. Lonely? How would it feel to visit family in Indiana and New York and not worry about anyone? Good? Yes, but it didn't tip the scales.

The crow, perched in the back of my mind, was cawing softly. I told my devoted vampire to take a midnight flight and search for his own fantasies. I googled the word knowingness. I liked the first definition - a state of awareness concerning the reality around you. It prompted a memory, a work meeting with a motivational speaker, strutting into the board room like a human peacock, with gold five inch heels, a bright blue handbag, a luminous yellow blouse and holding a water bottle in a hot pink case. Everything on her looked new. She oozed confidence. She claimed the moment. I had on a new pair of polka-dotted crew socks? I liked the second definition more - an intuitive feeling, transcending logic and intellect - a stream, glistening under moonlight, revealing the subtleties of movement, secreted beneath its surface.

My sister Linda, with her own intuitive gifts, was in Europe when Rachael gave birth to Jasmyne. She knew before I called her. She also heard her cat Spock, crying for help, when he was stuck in her bedroom. She was a visiting a friend, over a thousand miles away. My mother had a dream, the night before she died. The dream was very prophetic, giving her a distinct feeling that she and dad, who had passed over, were celebrating something together. She passed away the next day. It doesn't have to be anything intense or dramatic. It can be a thin strand of Divine Light, entering your soul, sparking a new thought or a much needed message. The bark I heard, told me what spirit already knew. Dog. Coming. Now.

Shaula Pearl was near, without flood lights or red carpets to announce her presence. It wasn't necessary. She was star material, just as she was. For the moment, she had no idea that a princess lived inside of her, and that soon, she would live in a small two story castle with her own spoon of cookie dough. Her joy run would manifest, her frightened body becoming strong and beautiful, and her muscles, rippling and flowing to the beat of a joy dance.

What I hold most dear, is what Wicca did. She died for the noble intention of saving Shaula Pearl, knowing that I would search for another dog. Not a replacement dog, but a dog. They must have been very good friends on the other side, or maybe dogs just know. They know what they need to do, and they do it.

Pooh is very intuitive. He is known for saying, "You can't stay in your corner of the forest waiting for others to come to you. You have to go to them sometimes." Jasmyne and I rose to his gentle wisdom. The next two weeks were grueling in the emotional sense.

We were team rescue, visiting numerous animal shelters and adoption websites. Nothing was pulling on my gut strings. Jasmyne was having a hard time trying to understand my gut, not that I blame her. Passing up so many hopeful dogs, was heart-wrenching, besides her tireless and very valid question. "Grandma. Is this the one? How about this one?" All I could manage to mumble was, "No. Not yet. I'll know her when I see her." The swell of tears had to be forced back may times, knowing that every dog we saw, needed to be enchanted.

As the third week dawned, and I still had no one to share my toast with, serendipity had its say. I was standing in the lobby of a hotel, that I am rarely in, and checking out a local workshop titled, the madness of the writers mind. It was me, all the way. A man with a mad hatter hat on, was passing out brochures, highlighting the sessions and who the speakers were. I was about to ask him for one, but instead, picked up a newspaper on his table. That was odd in itself, since I never read them. I opened it to the pet section, without much thought behind it. Nothing grabbed my attention, until I noticed a very small ad at the bottom of the page. "Animal rescue shelter. Please come and meet our adoptable dogs. You'll love them as much as we do."

The shelter was an hour and a half away. Jasmyne and I were on the road in minutes, sensing an adventure. The sky was a baby blue. Sweet, ripe oranges, from nearby orchards, scented our optimism. Life had a surgery taste to it. My dog was beautiful and gentle and had the kindest eyes. I could sense that. There was also a darkness around her, thick and oppressive.

My thoughts began spiraling around like wayward snowflakes, never quite clumping together. A turkey vulture flew overhead, reminding me of life, not death, that it recycles itself. I thought of my pet duck, hatched in my living room when I was sixteen, tagging me as a duck mother. Lack of feathers or webbed feet, didn't seem to be an issue. My hamster climbed out of my memory, resting in the pocket of my shirt. An hour later, an ambulance flew by with its ominous scream, jolting my thoughts to more unpleasant memories. My duck was eaten by a German Shepard who jumped our fence.

Some of us die in the warmth of a house while others fall out of doghouses. I shuddered, sensing my dog. I needed to find her.

I looked over at Jasmyne, who was staring out the window, absorbed in her own thoughts. My guess, she was thinking of pizza or how to escape the car and the crazy lady behind the wheel, smitten with dog paws. In my world, which she so kindly puts up with, dogs can do no wrong. They live in their dog heads, trying to blend in with the human world, a daunting task. Halloween costumes, pompom hairdos and painted toenails are love driven, but dogs want biscuits.

Twenty more minutes to the shelter. I would embrace the outcome, even if it went against everything I was feeling, and she wasn't there. If needed, I would declare myself a colossal loaf of banana nut bread, apologize to Jasmyne, and banish my gut to the corner for at least a month. In spite of my own doubts, lingering around like the persistent shadows of nightfall, I said to the dog ear, twitching inside my head, "I'm coming, sweetheart. Hold on." It was deja vu – Wicca, all over again.

I drove by the animal shelter twice, feeling frustrated, wondering why life had to make things difficult. Jasmyne told me to slow down and be calm, her young mind, filled with vision already. I took her advice. It appeared like magic on my next attempt, tucked off the road, away from the constant clattering of life - a safe harbor for lost souls. I slowed the car, knowing that I should never rush a journey.

The entrance was outdoors, with tables and chairs, packed with people and their newly adopted family members. Joyfulness jiggled the air, by not only the dogs, but their humans, all vibrating with uncontained love energy. It was a party of lost and found. It was a good day. We felt hopeful, approaching a small information window with a lady behind it, her large observant eyes, looking at both of us. We tagged her the owl lady. She handed me a short questionnaire. I could do this, having plenty of job application experience. Plus,

I was feeling positive that I could produce the desired answers. Although once, I was brutally honest, which you would think was important. I checked off 'yes,' I like to be alone. At some point, we all like to be alone? I wasn't hired. I was labeled anti-social and a loner. So I was careful but truthful. I had a distinct feeling, this shelter was serious about their adoption procedures and who they released their animals to. I respected that, having a neighbor once who appeared dog friendly. She played with her small dogs, chasing them around on her front yard, throwing Frisbees at them. When the fun was over, she put them in small cages and left them in her garage. Enough said.

The moment of truth had arrived. I couldn't pause it. The owl lady was going over my answers, tapping the application with a pencil eraser, making me nervous. The voice that lives in my head, allegedly on my side, was taunting me. "You're a hopeless romantic who has no magical powers of knowingness, and your gut finds great pleasure in fooling you. It lives to fool you." Jasmyne looked at me, smiling, making me feel better. "I think she's here, grandma," was all she said. I nodded, wordless. If Jasmyne was feeling it, there was a good chance it was true.

The owl lady was very accommodating, explaining the history of the shelter. Soon after, she opened the pearly gates, letting us in. At that moment, it looked easy. I would stroll in, feigning total poise and confidence in my flip flops and boring purse and find her. "We're here, and you're coming home with us," I declared, confidently. The universe was listening, granting my wish, but in its own alignment of divine timing. My plan for the day was being slightly twisted by the hands of fate.

We moved at a leisurely pace, with the owl lady at our side, who had offered to go with us. I wanted to be alone, zooming in on the dogs, listening for my girl, but I didn't say anything, knowing that owls are keepers of great wisdom. She ended up being a god-send, pausing at each confined area, explaining the story behind each set of eyes. She inquired often, if we wanted to sit with any of the dogs in the courtyard. "Not yet," was all I could say, staring at Jasmyne, wanting her to agree with me. She was silent.

Shelters have a panicky and anxious energy to them. At the same time, there is an undercurrent of hope from the animals themselves. You have to listen for it, otherwise, the negative feelings are overwhelming. I thought of a poem I had come across, eight years ago, encouraging me to become a vegetarian, along with Jasmyne. It left an impression. It was about cows. "They live and die and give much of themselves, the meat off their bones and their milk and their hide. Do they have nothing else of value? They do, but it's an invisible value and not everyone understands that." I felt moved to recite it, but I held my tongue, afraid that I would be tagged a pompous poet or a mystical cow person, obsessed with hoofs, not paws. But the poem had worth. The dogs, at the shelter, were treated horribly, because no one saw their value, or if they did, it made them angry.

We walked on, listening to the sad accounts of the dogs, who had either been homeless for unknown reasons, abandoned by their owners, or abused and rescued. All they wanted was to be loved. I felt mentally nauseous. Jasmyne was wonderstruck, her eyes wide as quarters. She was amazed and alarmed at the amount of animals who needed homes and who kept staring at us, that pleading, poignant stare that can melt a snowman. Their eyes were so telling. It was hard to look at them and impossible to pretend that you didn't feel their pain. If eyes are the portals to souls, it was here.

Finally, we arrived at the last row of dogs who were labeled special needs. I don't like labels, but at the very least, they provide information critical to the well-being of very distinct souls, beautiful as they are. These particular dogs had been less resilient to their abuse. Near the end of the row, I felt like a knowingness failure. I wasn't feeling it. Where was she? Maybe I was just pure nuts without the banana bread. Maybe I should rescue cows. I knew one thing, for sure. Hope doesn't go away unless you tell it to. The last cell was three feet away. We held hands, knowing that it was our last chance to celebrate the day with our new dog. I said to Jasmyne, "Look deep. Soften your eyes." My heart was pounding.

We slowed our pace, almost afraid to look. There was a dog, medium-sized, white with large black spots, sitting on her hide legs. Staring at nothing. Barely breathing. She was stone-still. Fear. It flowed from her like cold ripples. I had a cold flash. I felt her. She was beautiful. No, she was stunning. She had a charming design at the top of her head, in the shape of a peacock feather, reminding me of a third eye, staring upward. Her ears were large and black like a Shepherds. I thought of dark plum rose petals. Her fur was short and bright. The light in the shelter was strong, but she had a glow about her. I noticed her paws last. They were big and furry with pending kissable potential. She was my girl.

The owl lady spoke quietly, telling us her story. Lisa was her shelter name, given to her solely as a means of identification. She had been trapped on a ranch, owned by an animal hoarder. The day that animal rescue teams arrived, they found almost two hundred dogs who were in dire need of enchantment. Some of the dogs were roaming around free but severely neglected. Others were in cages. Every single one of them were either abused and neglected, sick or dead. Lisa was packed in a cage, along with many other dogs, starving and dehydrated. Gasoline had been found in their water bowls. They were hosed down off and on, a quick method of cleaning off blood and saliva. Also, they were cold, living outside. The bottom of her cage was a layer of ice.

When the owl lady ended her horror story, she asked me a question. "Would you like to sit with her in the courtyard?"

"Sure," I said, glancing at Jasmyne, who was bobbing her head up and down. I wasn't so sure that Lisa embraced the idea, who looked frozen to the spot. It didn't discourage the owl lady, who had a leash around her neck within seconds. To my surprise, Lisa followed her out, slow and stiff but without any visible resistance. When I took the leash, Lisa backed up as far as she could, putting her head down, her peacock eye staring at me. The owl lady assured me that she was okay. She guided us to a large, round cement bench, advising me to sit and relax my hold. Lisa didn't relax, and I didn't blame her. As far as she knew, I was a monster at the end of the leash, who could do anything that I felt like doing, and she would be helpless to prevent it.

Jasmyne wanted to hold her leash, but I wasn't sure it was a good idea. Lisa seemed to be wobbling on the edge of a panic attack. The owl lady agreed with Jasmyne, who confidently took the leash. Lisa became more compliant, still looking fearful, but her head was up, and she wasn't straining as much. I had forgotten how the energy of children is so open and loving. On some level, Lisa must have been feeling it. "I think she likes me," Jasmyne said, holding the leash with less tension than I had been. "I like her," she added. "She looks sweet. I think she will make the best dog in the whole world."

I love children. They see beauty in a potato bug. Jasmyne saw her value. Lisa was a living and breathing soul who deserved warmth, food, and shelter, and then layers of chocolate frosting – love, joy and respect at every opportune moment.

After about ten minutes, the owl lady put Lisa back in her cage. I expressed my feelings, that I felt positive, Lisa was the right dog for us and that she had tons of potential. The owl lady was pleasantly surprised, but advised us to look at few other dogs, already in the courtyard, who were up for adoption. It's always a blessing to have choices. We followed a long-haired sheep dog around, trying to get his attention. We sat with a tiny Maltese looking dog with spiked hair. She was sweet and making these little grunt sounds. We petted a black Shepard mix, who was a gorgeous dog with white feathery paws. There was also a lumbering sort of bear dog with large curls. He was adorable, sniffing everyone in sight, looking for his human.

The bear dog was tugging at my heart. The owl lady reappeared, wanting my opinion. Looking over at the bear, mentally apologizing to him, I told her that I wanted to adopt Lisa. This time, I got a hug.

She brought Lisa out to the courtyard, so we could sit with her while she gathered some paper work. We all sat together, staring at each other. No one said anything. We chilled more or less, processing the fact that we were looking at our dog, and our search had ended. At the same time, I knew that our journey was just beginning.

It was a beautiful day, ripe for enchantment. I could smell roses, but I didn't see any. I took it as a good omen, knowing how they vibrate with a high level of spiritual energy. A shaft of sunlight was pointing a golden finger at the building behind us, reminding visitors to think feline. It was filled to the brim with cats, waiting for their own personal scratching condos with catnip accessories. Also, there was a buzz in the air, beneath the surface of ongoing discussions. It was more on a vibrational level, in-between the notes of words and the space between breaths. It was love, the DNA of Divine Light, supporting all efforts to create joy, for each and every animal at the shelter.

I felt an exhilaration for life. I would give this to Lisa, against all odds. To the average eye, I made an impractical move, ignoring the cold facts. The dog I wanted was damaged, according to the norm, which is highly arguable anyways. In favor of spiritual insights, she had a peacock eye, and I had a gut eye, and Jasmyne had the eye of a child. It was a risk worth taking.

Soon, the owl lady emerged from her office with ice water and lemon. It looked like a celebration in progress, I hoped. She sat with us, citing a few examples of rescue dogs and their owners, that did not end happily ever after. She ended with a story about Bella, a special needs dog who had a few pending issues. The one deemed most critical, was her boundary issue. She didn't like to be kissed anywhere on the face. She didn't like to be touched on the face, either. In other words, don't get in her face. The family who adopted Bella, had a seven year old daughter who kissed Bella on her muzzle and got snapped at, the same day they brought her home. Bella was back at the shelter the next day. I can understand how the parents felt, concerning the safety of their child. I also appreciated the fact that they cared enough to adopt Bella, but they gave up on her. One day. One more day. Maybe it could have worked.

After the Bella story, the owl lady became very somber with me, saying her words slowly, pleadingly. "If you take her home, please don't bring her back. Commit to her one hundred percent." I said to her, "There's no way I will ever bring her back. She's family already." The owl lady was overjoyed, telling me that Lisa might never have been adopted. We hugged, no words necessary.

We stayed with Lisa, who was back in her cage, while the owl lady met with another family, briefly. I looked at my dog, who immediately backed into a far corner. She looked tilted with her hind legs at odd angles. I didn't know it yet, but odd angles were in her future, at least for the few first months, until she grasped the idea that she was safe. I had a feeling that enchantment would bloom, slow and gentle like an orchid, one petal at a time. I'd have to be patient. Knowing myself, I'd want to pry them open.

I was interviewed shortly after. In spite of the owl lady's initial excitement, concerning my decision, she wanted to be sure that I was the right person for Lisa. My heart was in my hands, willing to do whatever it took, for the privilege of adopting her. I passed without raising eyebrows, something I normally do, but the check list suited me. I lived alone. I had no other pets. I had a quiet household, no out-of-control chocolate parties. Also, I could make it home on a lunch break and take her out of her crate, for a short time, at least until she could manage the house without panic attacks. According to the owl lady, they would come, but not because she was frightened. At some point, she would fear that I wouldn't be coming back. It was nerve-racking, thinking about it. The only experience I had with panic attacks, was minimal. I swallowed an ice cube when I was young and thought I was dying. I panicked while my mother made soup, telling me calmly that it would melt it. She was right. I lived. I would have to remember that.

I was given one last word of advice, or maybe a warning. With Lisa, there was no guarantee that she would demonstrate any level of affection. I listened, but I couldn't imagine it. Still, her comment was slightly unsettling, putting a doubt in my head. Could I deal with that? I told myself, yes. If it was part of the journey, I didn't have a choice. It didn't feel right, to pick and choose what I wanted, when Divine Light was offering me something beautiful and in dire need of enchantment.

We left without her. It was hard, but I needed to get proof that my home owners association allowed dogs. I needed to doggie prove the house, including the backyard. There was a large hole in one of the corners, and a part of the fence was tilting backwards. I was told, very adamantly, that rescue dogs are magicians. If there's a way to escape, they will find it, and you won't catch them. The owl lady assured me, that she wouldn't be running from me. She would be running from her memories. I understood that. Memories can have long shadows. She then told me about a Chihuahua, who scaled a ten foot fence and was never found. "Leave nothing to chance," I was told on my way out. It made me nervous.

When I got home, I sat on the carpet, in the middle of the living room, scanning the house from a dog's point of view. I saw things. There was a nail, sticking out of the wall, low to the ground. There was a sharp edge to the coffee table. A glass dragon, sitting on a low shelf, was breakable. I stood up, scanning higher. I saw a window screen, torn slightly, and the cords from the window panes were dangling. A certain percentage of deaths occur every year from young children, tangled in loose cords. I fixed everything, having no clue that my list would get longer once she got home. When I arrived the following weekend, the staff at the shelter applauded. They didn't think I was coming back.

I headed straight to their pet store, buying everything I couldn't afford   beds and blankets, a variety of dog biscuits, two different colored leashes and a basket full of fluffy toys, which she ignored for the first year. I kissed my credit card, thankful that I had credit. I left the shelter that day, with my dog and my instruction list. It wasn't your ordinary list.

 Number One: When she was rescued, she was given the name of Lisa. Give her a new name. Use it often.

 Number Two: We are sending her home in a large crate, the same one in her cage. Encourage her to leave it, but never force the issue unless you have to.

 Number Three: Have patience. Wait for the trust to form. Wait for her to come to you. Never insist on anything.

 Number Four: Never scold her or punish her. Never raise your voice. It might be her first time inside a home. Clean up after her. Do it calmly and with gentle words.

 Number Five: Loud or sudden noises will frighten her. Don't say: "Poor baby. I'm sorry that scared you. Are you okay?" Instead, make a joke about it. You can say: "Did that ridiculous book fall? It doesn't bother us. We are super dogs." Teach her not to be afraid.

 Number Six: Leaving her in the house will make her feel abandoned. Leave and come back many times for the first week, helping her understand that you will always come back. Use the same words when you leave. You can say, "I'll be back. Also, place a treat where she can see it. It's great therapy, connecting a positive feeling with a human.

 Number Seven: She won't know that she's safe. She will pace back and forth, looking for a way out. Close doors!

 Number Eight: Encourage visitors to say her new name and talk to her quietly. Lay down the rules. Insist on respect. Protect her. You are the heart of her new life.

CHAPTER FIVE

BORN TO GLOW

"Dream lofty dreams, and as you dream, so you shall become."
James Allen

My pre-teen years were semi-normal, considering that I was fascinated with Frankenstein movies, green tree frogs, horny toads, insects, and science fiction books. My most intense obsession was Mister Toads Wild Ride at Disneyland. I would beg anyone, brave enough to accompany me, to let me drive. I would grip the steering wheel and go toad crazy.

I felt the ride. It was brimming with magic and adventure. The red devils, popping up with their devious grins and holding their plastic pitch forks, made me smirk. I would say under my breath, "You can't get me." Also, the heated air felt good. Overall, the ride made me feel happy and victorious. I always made it past them safely. Once, I rode on it ten times in a row. When I got home, I tried to build it in my backyard with large boxes, ropes and masking tape. It was a premonition. The day I adopted Lisa, I experienced the real wild ride on the Ventura freeway, North bound, with Lisa, panting in the back seat, heating up my Honda Civic.

For most of the ride home, she was sitting in her large crate without the top on, the only way it would fit in my car. I kept a good eye on her, figuring if she panicked, I would grab her leash, holding her steady. Jasmyne was not with me to help. The owl lady was very insistent that I take her home by myself and not to make any stops. It was a little intimidating. Trying to maintain an air of confidence, I whispered, with a fair amount of force, some command driven mantras. "You will not mind wander. You will not think of things that haven't happened. Love is everything. You will always remember that. You can do this."

Lisa was frozen, staring out the window. I would have ignored chocolate for a week, to know what she was thinking. I dropped the mantras, wondering if I sounded threatening, more like a snake hissing than a human. I talked to her instead, telling her that I liked her name, that it was a lovely name but for someone else. I told her about the bunnies, and Mesa and Wicca, romping around the house, but not in the physical sense. She ignored me, not surprisingly. She didn't have any reason to pay attention. I kept talking to her anyways, looking for anything doggie, an ear twitch, a huff. All I could see was desperation. There was no way for her to understand, at the moment, that she was safe and that I loved her. If I dropped to my knees, with offerings of dog bones wrapped in sardines, soaked in olive oil, it wouldn't have made a difference. Love, at the very least, is only a word. I love you. Smack. You made me do it. You wouldn't stop barking.

I was beginning to feel angry, thinking about what we do to each other, but anger serves no purpose. It's spilt energy. I needed to concentrate on her healing. I swore to myself that I would pull out the parts of her that were hidden, the jewels of her soul, glittering and glowing, telling me what she liked, what made her feel joyous. I focused on color, releasing a display of pink energy, happy vibrations, spreading into the backseat like silent fireworks. I asked angels for divine guidance, helping me to enchant her, sensing that I would need more than a plan, a journal and my chocolate muses. I begged for creative inspiration, knowing that different ways of looking at things would be needed. If she pooped in the house, as I had been so delicately forewarned, I would call it ice cream. My challenge was coming.

To make something manifest at a phenomenal speed, close to warping time, you have to feel it, deep in the marrow of your bones.

I poured out the pink, flooding the car with it, throwing imaginary red roses in the back seat for extra support. In flower language, they send out a warm flow of energy, vibrating with love and strength and a passion for life. I added bouquets of heart shaped balloons and the scent of raspberry chocolate. If she wasn't feeling it, on a subliminal level, I would have been mystified. Dogs have an incredible ability to sense things beyond human perceptions. They can smell individual ingredients in your soup. Also, believing in the power of words, as living entities, I sang one of the most light-hearted songs I could think of, The Happy Birthday Song. In a way, it was her birthday. It was a day to celebrate new beginnings. New journeys. She would have milk and honey and drink out of goblet if she felt like it. I was doing something right. The first mile on the freeway seemed effortless.

The second mile was scary. The real wild ride had begun. Lisa plunged into the front seat without warning, her legs, scrambling for a foot-hold. They came to a quick stop on the gear shift panel. Her massive paws, visibly kissable now, moved seconds later, hitting the front panel, bashing knobs and switches. My radio went on. My air went off. My hot flash went on. It triggered something. She froze, looking out the front window. Her arms, above the glove compartment, were as stiff as thin boards.

I tried to remain calm and not move, except to manage the steering wheel, but I did glance at her quickly. She looked so frightened. I whispered to her, "It's okay, Lisa. You're safe." She remained where she was, making slight adjustments with her paws. Then, she spun around like a ballet dancer, landing in her crate with a loud thump. I snapped a muscle in my neck, twisting my head around, searching for the end of her leash. I wanted to moan but thought twice about it. Moaning could be a bad memory. The fires were out, for the moment. She was quiet, staring out the window, panting heavily.

The remainder of the drive home was think time. Dog brains. Animal behavior. I was more adept at baking and being joyous. I worried about how easy it would be to misinterpret her and make horrendous mistakes. At the same time, being the fool on the hill, stepping off without safety nets or instructional pamphlets, I was hopeful. I would charm the mouse out of a snakes belly - the mouse being her fears. I was trusting, more than ever, that my angelic support team, my shimmering dot team, and my dogs, with their wings and halos, would lead me and guide me on this yet to be enchanted journey. My prayer was simple. Help me to open her heart, so she can free her soul. Sing like a wild bird. Fly to never-imagined places and grin, for the sweet and simple joy of being alive.

Mesa and Wicca were loved effortlessly and without a plan. I knew that with Lisa, I would have to create one, even if it was written in the moment. I would have to capitalizing the word trust. You trust if you receive the same message, day after day. I would add an expectancy clause, so she would expect the same behavior from me, under any circumstance. "Hi. Lisa. I'm home. Why are you hiding in the closet? I'm the one with the bad day! Oh, sorry. Come get your dinner. I love you." If I was truly having a bad day, I would have to leave it outside.

Healing and trust are inter-reliant, holding hands, walking in the chill of the morning, waiting for the sun to pour out of its own honey pot, into the sleeping sky, warming the backs of birds and the icy cheeks of wild hares. The sun is always at the horizon, peering into the world. You trust it. You don't worry about it. You know, beyond a doubt, that it will rise in the morning, signaling in the dawn. Lisa needed to believe, at the very least, that I was someone she could rely on, all of the time. Day or night. Awake or asleep.

I also knew, I would have to be very clear with my words. Language can be so confusing. "Don't bark. It's my friend. Bad dog!" An hour later, "Bark. I don't know who it is. Good dog!" Also, I would have to watch her constantly, knowing that she would express to me, in subtle ways, what she needed and wanted. "I want to sniff you, but don't touch me." She told me that for the first few months. Every moment of our time together, was crucial to her healing and needed to be love-based. Dogs live in the moment. For example, they don't worry about what's for dinner or when it's coming. When it appears, they eat. They don't think, "Whew. I wondered about it, because it was late yesterday." I had a lot of work to do.

Glancing at Lisa only fueled my view on enchantment. Love and joy is for all souls, for two feet, four paws, two wings, four claws. It doesn't matter. A soul is a soul. The outer sheath makes no difference. Lisa, with her special needs label, would be counted among the enchanted. Her value would glow. I would love this girl until she felt it. I thought of a friend, years ago, who reflected the embodiment of divine love. She had a beautiful baby girl, who was born blind, deaf and mentally challenged. She had no idea what was going on behind her little face, and it didn't matter. She loved her baby and took her everywhere she went. Her baby didn't live long, but she lived in the arms of someone who cared the world about her. Love stands alone at the end of the day. It lets in the magic.

With that in mind, I arrived home, feeling that I was teetering on the edge of a whole new threshold, crafted by unseen powers, very magical and far beyond my expectations. I said a quick prayer to the angels, asking them to oversee our first night together, sensing how much I would need their assistance. For now, I had to attend to earthly matters. Lisa was home. I hoped to get her out of the car without alerting the entire neighborhood. Sometimes, thinking is detrimental. I opened the back door, holding her leash. Lisa did the dog thing. She jumped out of the car, landed on my feet, and then she followed me to the front door. I was stunned and relieved, and I didn't trust any of it.

Her calmness, her princess composure, was a red flag. Her eyes were darting back and forth, and her mouth was open. She was beginning to wheeze a little, and a faint whistling sound was coming out of throat. I had a bad feeling about this. I questioned the owl lady's advice. Tether her to my waist for the first few days. If I didn't, she could have full blown panic attacks, injuring herself. Still, it didn't sound very dog-friendly, attaching myself to Lisa who believed in monsters.

I made my first mistake. When we entered the house, I dropped the leash. Lisa knew she was free. She took off, pacing the living room. It was a frantic pace, wild and tense, reminding me of caged jaguar that I had seen at a zoo, its muscular body, bursting with coiled up stress. I kicked myself mentally, mad that I wasn't a better listener. Now, I had to catch her and avoid what I had sworn never to do - frighten her even more than she was.

Acting purely on instinct, I followed her in the most non-aggressive manner I could think of, before the big bunny position. I crawled. She paused for a few seconds, staring at me. It bought me time. I took hold of her leash, but lost it a few seconds later, watching her fly toward the window. Recovering the leash, with my heart doing double time, was challenging. I pretended to be calm, tying it to my waist and walking into the kitchen, expecting a tug of war. I was surprised, again. Lisa followed me, but she wasn't happy about it. Her legs were stiff, so she was walking with an odd gait. Her neck was bent at an odd angle with one eye staring at me. "What have we gotten ourselves into," I whispered, wondering if my voice frightened her.

We lack wings. We rarely possess the panorama view of an eagle, seeing miles down a river or around corners, but we can see with our hearts. I looked at Lisa, as open and transparent as I've ever been. I wanted her to sense me, how much I cared about her. Then, I listened. She said, "I'm afraid, but I'm here. Don't hurt me. Don't leave me." Her body trembled.

"I will never leave you," I told her, smiling as slight as a crescent moon. I couldn't do much better. There was such a deep sadness to her.

Dinner seemed like a safe activity. I wanted to make rice, so boiling water was a given. The box said it was a five minute experience, but with a dog attached to your jeans, it was more like twenty. Finding the pan, deep into the belly of the lower shelf, was challenging normally, but squatting with Lisa was a little thought provoking. We were teeth level with each other.

Moving around the kitchen was scary, sensing how easily it would be to injure her. Stepping on her paws or losing my balance, seemed inevitable. I walked slowly, staring at my feet. My child development kicked in. Unintentional injury is the leading cause of death in young children, and one-third of these are at home. Household appliances are listed as one of the lethal enemies. I placed the pot on a back burner, feeling I had covered my bases. Just in case, I secured the end of her leash, that was tied to my jeans, around the leg of my kitchen table. The X factor is forever present. It is the element of chaos, of the unexpected, throwing that wrench into your best laid plans. Hot blistering water would be one of them. The other one was about to happen.

Dinner was an hour away, but I was hungry. It didn't feel right, eating in front of Lisa, so I offered her some gourmet canned dog food with chucks of salmon, plus a biscuit. She looked away. I had been forewarned that she might not eat, at least for the first day. Fear overrides everything. I felt guilty anyways, pouring myself a small bowl of cereal. In doing so, I became acutely aware of sounds - the ruffling of paper, inside the cereal box, and the silverware, clattering against each other. She flinched at everything.

In spite of our initial home coming fiasco, I was feeling optimistic. The rice was boiling and my cereal, half eaten. The feeling was premature. My elbow smacked the box of rice off the counter. When it hit the floor, Lisa exploded. I learned the meaning of the term, adrenalin rush. Lisa pushed backwards with such force, she tore off the table leg. I froze. She froze, and the table came crashing down. She plunged into the living room in blind fear, with me at her heels, throwing myself on the leash and then running with her, so she wouldn't choke herself. She stopped soon after, panting wildly. Number five on the list - turn a frightening situation into something comical. It was worth a try. "Excuse me?" I said to the box of rice. "Did I tell you that it was okay to fall off the counter? And don't think I didn't see you, elbow." She looked better. Her tongue wasn't hanging out as far.

We chilled for a few minutes. I studied her. She looked fragile, with her rib cage so pronounced. Her legs were thin and brittle looking. I feared they could snap in half. Her display of strength was her body, dumping stress hormones into her blood stream, giving her super powers. Still, it amazed me, the amount of force she exhibited. My table had thick legs.

A piece offering was in order. I offered her some fish, holding it under her nose. She stared at it blankly. I tried once more. She sniffed at it this time, barely twitching her nose, but I saw it. I wanted to put the word sniff on a button, on a poster board, tattoo it on my forehead. I didn't care where, I was so excited. It was dog-normal and a statement from the soul of my silent girl. "I will sniff, but that's it."

The rice was ready to eat, but I wasn't hungry anymore, at least for food. I was hungry for words. I sat with her on the kitchen floor, holding a notebook and a pen, feeling sniff and buoyant. I wrote her things and then I read them to her while she ignored me....The day is headed home, gathering her sleepy souls, cradling them in her grassy arms, in her sun spun body, now splashed with the first shadows of twilight, as she slips quietly into her ashen gown.

I looked at Lisa, who was sitting on her hind legs, stiff as a porcelain statue. Unbeknownst to me, a year later, a psychic friend informed me of something very enlightening, over a wickedly delicious black forest pound cake, the mind remembering all inspiring moments. She told me, "Your dog loves it when you read to her. She always has." I realize now, more than ever, that our most seemingly insignificant moments, have hands, carrying us when needed.

Without knowing the extent of it, our time together, on the kitchen floor, was therapeutic, and perhaps, planted the first seeds of enchantment. I was writing and reading, always a healing balm. Lisa was listening, out of no choice of her own, but she was in a quiet and non-threatening place, a least physically. I continued on.... Our souls make us sky-riders, you and I. Our hair, tangled with star patterns. Our feet, running with God's mind across the cosmos. Our flesh, now luminous with the crimson fires of creation, melts away. We are loose from mortal limits, flying with diamond crushed wings through moonlit canyons and mountains glowing with sunbaked marigolds, as tall as trees. There is everything we can imagine, away from the edges of the earth, where we try to remember who we are and what it feels like to walk barefoot on the rich, deep soil of our dreams.

I felt calmer, but Lisa was miles away, swimming in her memories, and it wasn't anywhere pleasant to imagine. She glanced at me quickly and looked away. I was the fool-hearted enemy, armed with paper and the imaginings of my wild soul. Most likely, she was waiting for me to hurt her. I looked around at the kitchen, from the vantage point of the floor. Weird, shiny objects. Walls that trapped. A metal trashcan, unfamiliar and dangerous. I suddenly realized, I had to see the world through her eyes. I thought of toddlers. The slide goes down in the eyes of adults. The toddler sees it from every possible angle, usually going up. Everything hinges on the reality inside of our own minds. I needed to get inside of hers, and quickly.

It was tempting to do nothing for the entire evening but share thoughts, mine at least, but it wasn't conducive to either of our needs. I needed the sanctity of my bedroom, my laptop, and my pajamas, and she needed to get into a routine. I stood up, cracking a knee. She flinched, but she also made a sound, beyond sniff. It was more of a raspy inhale with a snort attached. Normally, I would have considered it cute, but in reality, it was fear-based. Everything was. How frightening I must seem to her. She didn't know how to interact with a human or that it was even possible. She didn't know what it felt like to be given an extra biscuit for just being wonderful.

Pooh understood. "He thought how sad it was to be an animal who had never had a bunch of violets picked for him."

A long winter's night was ahead of us. Lisa was in her crate staring at her paws. I was sitting on the couch staring at my feet. I turned on the TV which only added to the weirdness of the hour. I usually avoid it, unless I can find a good, respectable scary movie without torture. TV is creepy enough by itself, an object of great luminosity without a mind but with its own brand of enchantment. It pulls you in and then you sit by it for hours, staring at it. Tonight, it would serve as a good zone out. A few minutes went by slowly. Neither of us were in the mood to be empty headed. I was too worried about her to relax. Lisa was calm but resonating with nervous energy. She was, by far, the worst off. I knew, I was safe.

The electronic-pretend life form had seconds to live. I dimmed the lights and lit candles. I talked to her, telling her how pretty she looked, how I loved her big furry paws and that she was really a princess, and I would prove it to her. I told her that we should sleep and dream. She had a warm crate now, and it would be a good experience. I explained to her that our bedroom was upstairs and how we could arrive there, safely. "You will be in the crate, all safe and snug, and I will be dragging you up the stairs. If that doesn't work, I will tilt you out of the crate, as gently as I can, wrap my arms around your middle like a hug and walk you up." I didn't sound friendly, no matter how I said it.

The crate wasn't behaving. With Lisa in it, crunched up against the back side, it was hard to maneuver. It pounded up the first step. She panicked, scrambling to the front of the crate at mock speed, hitting her head on the door. I cringed. Maybe, if I had moved the bench press and barbells out of the garage, I might have used them and this would have been a piece of cake. I had no option but to slide her out. It went smoothly, but I had to tilt the end of the crate up, higher than I anticipated. After that, I wrapped my arms around her belly, and we walked up, six legs at a time. Half way up, a strange sound bubbled up out of throat. It was the beginning of a gurgle, soon to manifest. I tried to ignored it, focusing on the dark chocolate fiber bar in my nightstand. At least, the walk up was easier than I thought. She was only thirty-five pounds, underweight for her size.

She followed me downstairs, tethered to my wrist, to retrieve the crate. It didn't seem that surprising when I thought about it, how she followed me without any intense outbursts of fear. There wasn't any fight in her. Soon after, I sat at my writing desk, with Lisa behind me. I was strongly advised to keep my normal routine going, if at all possible. I was trying, but she was so nervous. I couldn't think of anything but her fear. It was ice cold.

I put her in her crate, earlier than I had planned. There, she would have a clear view of me and what I was doing, without being forcibly involved. Writing seemed like a safe and nonthreatening activity, sure to become familiar. My evenings were very habitual. I come home, eat and write. The weekends are similar. I am home. I eat and write. I have moments of normalcy. I get dressed, go somewhere, come home, and then eat and write. Lisa would get to know the back of my head.

I opened a file. Lisa sniffed loudly. Writing took a back seat. Love came tumbling in. I knew, at that very moment, my journey with Lisa was spiritual. It was grounded in leashes and crates, but the soul of it was orchestrated by the harmonious and melodic voice of Divine Light. I had felt that in the car, pulling into the driveway, but I couldn't put a name to it. It all came together that first night.

I looked at her, still as midnight - a quiet and reflective hour but very powerful, submerged in the silky whisperings of the spirit world. It was Lisa, all the way. She was full of secrets and messages, yet to be discovered. I also felt such an odd feeling of completion, not in the sense of an ending, but traveling for years, experiencing many journeys, and then suddenly, having her here in the room with me.

I felt the importance of the hour and how it was about to adjust the very angles of my life. My spiritual chiropractor had arrived.

I looked back at my laptop, feeling the guilt of a writer. If you don't write, staring at your own electronic enthrallment of choice, a part of your soul, empties. A pound of fudge doesn't help. I tried again. It was a healthy choice. You burn over one hundred calories in an hour, sitting and writing, depending on your weight. I argued with a blank page. I couldn't focus. Lisa was here in the room with me. Lisa was in my life. It felt familiar. It felt exciting and overwhelming, but mostly, it felt right.

Promises were stacking up. I would listen to her. It was more potent than hearing. I would find her, the real Lisa, the puppy Lisa, born happy, and I would stomp on her fears. Strangle her nightmares. If hell was there, I would push it to a place where it was weak and ineffective. Nothing with negative intentions would have squatter rights, if I had anything to say about it.

I made a grand effort to sleep. It was a wasted endeavor. Lisa was in her crate making little sounds, and they didn't sound happy. She would moan softly and then she would puff, exhaling a fair amount of air. She squeaked once. She snuffed. But most often, she whined. It was heart breaking. I wanted to sit by her and tell her that her eyes were as sweet as M&M's, and that one day, she would be served toast on a fancy paper plate.

The owl lady, with her cache of gems, her doglike pearls of wisdom, had advised me, with unwavering conviction, that when she whines at night, do not say or do anything. When she stops, for even a second, praise her for being such a good girl. Reward positive behavior. It works like magic.

I wasn't sure I could do it. I transport moths off walls, putting them outside. I relocate snails off sidewalks. I had to remind myself, this wasn't an "I" situation. I balanced it out, going overboard on the praise part. She was silent, ten minutes later. It backlashed but only on me. I was so excited, I couldn't sleep. Besides, my writing muse was singing to me like a seductive sea nymph, luring me out of bed. I took the bait, realizing that it was the perfect time to hunt down her new name. I was sure of only one thing. She wasn't a Lisa.

There is a power in your name. It defines who you are. It arouses memories. You hear it across a room. It should make you feel beautiful and strong. In some cultures, you're given a birth name. When you get older, you can change it. I like that. We out-grow who we are many times, and we can definitely outgrow our names.

There is a tribe in Africa that has my heart. The birthday of a child, is not the day the child enters the world. It is the day the child becomes a thought in the mother's mind. When that happens, she walks off by herself, finding a place to sit, away from everyone. After that, she listens. At some point, she hears the song of her child, and it becomes the child's name. She teaches it to her husband, and they sing it to the child during birth. The song is then taught to the family and the villagers. The name is more than a way to get your attention. It's a beautiful sound.

Lisa needed her own sound, her own distinct name, celebrating herself. I combed through websites, looking at a variety of options, from Greek to Hebrew to Italian names. I tried unusual and mysterious dog names. I tried princess and goddess names. I became obsessed with names. I tore open a stash of dark chocolate in my pajama drawer, saving it for a severe attack of writer's block. The endorphins poured in. I searched for the names of stars. The first website that popped up, had a list of ninety-one names. She didn't look like a Betelgeuse or a Spica, and she didn't have the right look for a Sirius or a Polaris. I liked Rana, but it meant frog. Maybe if she was small and jumpy. I liked Capella, but it meant she-goat. I couldn't justify it.

It was the witching hour. Midnight would have to pull through with its legendary magic. Somebody with the powers to enchant, must have been helping. I tried one more website. Half way down the list, was the star, Shaula. There was something about it, the way it sounded, the way it felt. I repeated it a few times, afraid to look at its meaning, anticipating something weird like hip-bone.

I got lucky. Shaula was a large star in the constellation Scorpio, at the end of its tail. The tail is up, a good omen for the future of her own tail. Also, Shaula is one star, in a pair of stars, called The Stinger. It related to her. Sting can be an acute mental pain. I read further. Shaula is the 24th brightest star in the night sky. One day, it will explode as a supernova, an event so powerful, it will be visible in another galaxy. The name fit her. I wanted her to glow and sparkle, light up her crate, light the room, the house, the universe. She was destined to be a light, exploding out of herself in a flood of joy. I was feeling it. Her joy run was coming.

I had no idea that her name wasn't complete. The following night, we were standing in the backyard under a full moon, getting used to each other, although it was tether enforced. I was talking to her, in support of my carpet, trying to convince her that dirt and weeds enjoy the results of bladder relief. I was side-tracked. I looked at her, awestruck. Her fur was glowing under the moonlight, as bright as virgin snow. The moon had christened her Pearl. Welcome home, Shaula Pearl.

CHAPTER SIX

THE QUIET FIRES OF HOPE

*"If you are going to walk on thin
ice, you might as well dance."*
An Eskimo Proverb

"Good morning, Shaula Pearl," I said, with a touch of panache, bowing deeply and spreading my arms wide, embracing the stillness of the room and the quietness of my lovely dog. I adored the sound of her new name. I used it numerous times that morning, waking up the bedroom, opening the blinds, shaking out my throw rug and watching a quarter fly out of it. I grabbed it, appreciating its value. Four quarters add up to a soda. I showed it to Shaula Pearl, who shuffled around in her crate, turning her backside to me. "Okay. I get that," I said, sitting by her, looking at her tail. "Give it time. You will enjoy the small pleasures of the day, I promise you."

I was grateful it was Sunday, the Sun's Day, a bright and hopeful day. The energy of Sunday is success, faith, and eternal optimism. There is also a dignity to the day. I wanted Shaula Pearl to feel that, ultimately - the sacredness of her soul, the worth of it. For the moment, I wanted her out of the crate, exploring her new world, full of cinnamon scented candles, freshly baked brownies, and me, always happy to see her. I believed in the power and enchantment of joyful encounters.

I wasn't sure where to begin, but freedom was a good start. I opened her crate door, sliding her out, only to see her run back in. We played slide about every hour. I tethered her off and on, walking her around the house and out in the backyard, determined to help her locate her relief zone. Bathroom. Praise. Treat. It didn't seem like a hard concept, except with Shaula Pearl, it was. Concepts are rooted in your own private experiences. She didn't have the mental networks to hook into my plan. In my world, it was - You do this and you get something yummy. You get yummy no matter what. In her world, it was - You do this and it doesn't matter. Nothing matters.

Your inner world doesn't change overnight, even if your outer world does. She was safe with new things to consider, but inside of her mind, there was a wall of fear. At the same time, the sun was out and the weeds were thriving. I saw promise. Shaula Pearl saw an ordinary gray lizard zip across the dirt near one of her paws. She tracked it methodically, moving her head back and forth, as it scurried in a patch-work fashion across the wood planks. I was stunned at the amazing normalcy of the moment. The ordinary had become extraordinary. If my life with Shaula Pearl had a sub-title, that would be it.

The day was now tagged, lizard Sunday. I stood with Shaula Pearl for a long time, enjoying her silent company. She eventually sat down, stiff as ever, on a warm patch of dirt, putting her head down, shivering a little. Memories were there, haunting her. I sat on a patch of wild grass, feeling grateful that I had found her, that I had listened. I felt positive, that her deep suspicions about me, and her high level of unease, would diminish. I couldn't imagine it any other way. I shivered along with her. There was a shift in the air, a slight breeze out of nowhere. Enchantment was brewing.

Spirit was lapping at my feet, leaving me gems glittering between my toes. To the mundane eye, it was gravel, but I saw differently. I looked up, and the sky seemed dreamlike, a sprawling thought from a divine mind, a numinous blue, glowing behind garlands of white clouds, the wings of angels, folding into the earth realms. I felt threads, thin and silvery, connecting the energies of all souls, the weeping of the willow, the melodies at midsummer, from birds claiming their trees, and the long, cold sigh of a winter night. The soul of the world was whispering. I heard love. It must be what everything is made of.

Shaula Pearl had popped out of her pain, long enough to see the world, a blessed lizard. Celebrations were in order. She must have agreed. She ate a small amount of food and drank some water. I was ecstatic, silently. In truth, I wanted to set up a loud speaker and a microphone and proclaim to the neighborhood, what an amazing wonder dog she was. The homeowners association would have sent me a warning in the mail that my outburst of joyful behavior was not allowed, and it would go into my file.

The second night wasn't much different, except for the fact that she was sideways in her crate, with her body folded up like an origami dog. After a while, she moved, stretching her front legs out as much as possible and putting her head by the crate door. Glancing at me every few minutes, surprised me, but it was anxiety based. I felt like the legendary Medusa, the hideous human female with venomous snakes on her head, instead of hair. It wasn't far from the truth. My hair looked a mess, left to its own maneuvers without a flat iron. She didn't care, now or forever. Appearances would never be important to her. Actions would be.

Tonight, it was all about surviving, not thriving, at least in her head. She was trembling sporadically. I did everything I could think of that would make her more comfortable. I removed the lightbulbs from my ceiling fan, except for one. The room was softer. I played soothing, meditative music. I scented the air with lavender incense. I then sat by her crate, facing her, so she could bond with the other side of me. I didn't say anything, and I didn't look at her. I wanted her to get used to my presence. Eventually, I opened the crate door and sat on the bed. She didn't move. Oddly, when I sat at my desk, she came out of her crate and went back in. It was a moment, brief as it was, that spoke of strength and resolve. The divine intervention of two dogs were involved. Mesa and Wicca were there, elbowing her to come out, and without a doubt, grinning at her.

Later in the evening, on a gut feeling, I placed candles by her crate and sat by her, meditating. When I finished, I said, "Good night, Shaula Pearl, the prettiest girl." She must have liked it. I saw something in her eyes, a faint spark of recognition, a murky twinkle, fighting for its life. It was the beginning of her song, weak as it was. I shivered. Two nights were not enough time for enchanting a soul. The spiritual realms were moving in swiftly with their mysterious ways, regardless of the earthly constraints of time. It shouldn't have surprised me. If you reside in a place where clocks are nonexistent, life becomes one continual flow, a revolving door, with dogs coming and going without calendars – where there is no such thought, remotely analogous to the word impossible.

Like we all do, I live with the face of clocks, watching me, reminding me that I have to be somewhere or do something. It doesn't feel right. Just the same, I had five days off. The first week was pandemonium in its purest state. Chaos ruled, but it's not always a bad thing. It can be a positive word, an exalted state, connected to acts of creation. Gas and dust collapsing to begin the makings of a star. The mixing of light and shadow, creating the tranquil musings of twilight, or the chaos inside of us before we figure it out.

After chaos, there will be calm. It became another mantra. I repeated it often. I visualized it. Dust settling. Light filtering in. Shaula Pearl, standing in the middle of it, glowing enchantingly. We weren't there, yet. Every morning, Shaula Pearl ate and threw up, found her special relieve spot, somewhere in the house, and paced back and forth, looking for a way out. If she wasn't pacing, she was in her crate. She wouldn't leave it, unless I slid her out. The owl lady's advice rang true. "Don't let her zone out anywhere. She won't make any progress." I believed that. There are days where you want to embrace numb, crawl under your bedsheets and snub the day.

The second week, I had to go back to work. I was confronted with questions about my new dog. No one remembered her name, so she was renamed. "How's your um, you know, your new dog, your different dog." I fought back. "Hi, different person. How's your um, day off request coming? I said that once, but it was in my office with the door shut.

I knew that nothing was meant to be offensive. There was concern for my new, different dog. I told a few people about her in more detail. I got an array of responses, all with good intentions. "Strange. She sounds strange," was a common one. One syllable words became popular. "Wow. Crazy. What?" Also, there was the depressed look. "She has it way harder than me," I would say, with sympathetic nods of the head and offers to buy me shots of expresso. I thought about that one. Did I look dazed? Exhausted? If I did, so did Shaula Pearl, along with scared and joyless.

By the end of the week, the comments slowed. Only one, took me by surprise. A previous supervisor walked into my office, whom I hadn't seen in a few months. She looked at Shaula Pearl, who was now on my peg board and my computer screen, and said, "I've heard all about her. This might be too much for you. Didn't your dog pass away? Maybe you need a dog that is more - normal?"

"I was never into normal," I said, with a slight grin. I forgave her. Love was enchanting me.

After she left, I thought about the word normal. Society aligns the word normal with mainstream everything. The majority rules, from hair color to the acceptable length of your toenails. What about the individual ruling? If you had a potbellied pig for a pet and a crocodile, would your neighbors call you abnormal? If you felt normal with it, would it still be abnormal? Shaula Pearl is who she is, because of what she endured. If you lived in a scary room without an exit door, you would have issues.

I have to admit, the week was odd by any standard. Instead of Starbucks, my lunch hour was chopped up into minutes. Twenty minutes home. Fifteen minutes to slide Shaula Pearl out of her crate, walk her outside, give her a biscuit, and gently push her back in. Twenty minutes back to work. Five minutes in the restroom. Evenings were less of a routine, but not by much. I would tether her to my waist, walk around the backyard and the house, and then sit with her on the rug, telling her about my day, minus any well-intentioned but weird remarks. After a half hour of rug bonding and eating, we would go upstairs. Candles. Music. Typing. Meditating. Bed. If I had ever yearned for order and structure in my life, Shaula Pearl called it in.

It was day seven, wonderfully abnormal. It came and went quickly, most likely, from a schedule developing and my life becoming more habitual than it had been. At night, I performed my check list – double check the latch on the crate door, blow out the candles, feet on the mattress, check in with the dots and say a good night to all three of my dogs. Mesa and Wicca are alive. Dead is an earthly term.

Shaula Pearl was quiet that night. Her heart wrenching sounds were history. I was thankful for that and for everything I had, and what I didn't have, didn't matter. On an impulse, I said goodnight to my bed. Bed is a gift. My house burned down, thirteen years ago, from a gas leak in the garage. House fires remind you, how amazingly wonderful your own bed feels or a pair of socks. The worst part of the entire experience, was going from chocolate to no chocolate in ten minutes. With that thought, I said goodnight to my dark cocoa bar with 200 mg of potassium in one square. Healthy choices are important.

Minutes later, a loud smack startled me, throwing my heart off. Shaula Pearl had spun around in her crate. I crawled over, noting how crawl was now normal, and peeked into the side bars. She jerked massively, bumping her head. Then, she began digging with her paws. I backed off, concerned. What was she doing? Night terrors? Trying to escape?

Thank the angels, it only lasted a few seconds, ending in a loud grunt. Grunt was better than a groan. I crawled back to bed, worried to death about her mental state. What was she thinking? I could ask her mentally, but I didn't think, in her state of mind, she would listen. Calling Julia, in the morning, was an option, but I had a strong feeling, I knew what she would say. Shaula Pearl is thinking about everything. She has balled up energy. Maybe it's a memory. Maybe she's digging, because it feels good. I answered myself, but knowing the universe, an unplanned meeting with my friend, was sure to be in my future.

I love blaming things on my DNA. Odd thoughts, floating around in my genetic inheritance, is a good excuse for being plagued by them. I laid in bed, musing over the word, think. The process of thought, of being lost in it, intrigues me. Your soul hears you. It is a mute and silent language. You can go anywhere in your thoughts. Animals have thoughts. Nature has thoughts. You can feel them. A meadow of buttercups, little sapphires, fills you with yellow. They send you light. You feel light. A pot of Pansies, gem colored divas of the flower world, tell you to think joy, to do things that make you happy. The glow of a Luna moth, sailing in the dark waters of the night, with its sea-green wings, tells you to grow wings and travel to worlds you've never been to.

Shaula Pearl was thinking, I was sure of it. I flashed on Wicca, who taught me the absence of thought and how pleasurable it can be. She was good at it, when the car window was down, even a few inches. She would smell the wind, scented with a million unseen things, with her tongue flapping and her eyes glazing over. Humans refer to it as living in the moment. It should be an exalted state, right along with chaos. Perhaps everything is an exalted state - god inspired doorways, opening around us all the time, leading us to our higher selves, our most vibrant selves.

I was tired, but I couldn't sleep. I was too open to her, at this point. I felt her from the inside-out. I tried meditating in bed, sweeping out my ever-distracting thoughts with a spectral broom. It worked for a while. I could feel myself drifting off but then cows came in without heads. An internet article I had read recently, on the emotions of cows, conjured up the image. The author was sharing his opinion that cows are not mindless mechanical moos. He had visited a ranch, noticing the strange, moaning sounds of the cows, as he left his car. He noted their odd behavior, their wild eyes and their overall suffering. The rancher explained their behavior. All of their calves had been taken away to be slaughtered, and they were next.

I rocked myself to sleep, curling up in a ball. Holding in the pain. So many animals who are not allowed the right of a joy run.

I awoke to something very enchanting, perhaps transcendental, and definitely not normal. The pale, delicate light of the morning, was cutting through the blinds, lighting the top of Shaula Pearl's head, glowing her peacock feather. I was spellbound. If this was the epitome a third eye experience, I wasn't about to argue. I looked her in the eye, her sun-drenched eye. She looked back at me, strong like a dog goddess. I heard her soul, snug and warm, dancing in the zebra light, whispering to her that she was beautiful.

Feeling charmed and spellbound, wasn't conducive to earth bound work issues. I wanted to luxuriate in it, roll around in it like a pig in mud. I was tempted to call work, explaining that I didn't feel normal, that I was having weird thoughts, maybe fever induced. It wouldn't have worked. My staff would have said, "But that's you?" Instead, I turned on the heat. That was odd in itself. It wasn't a cold morning. Maybe the whole world had woken up under a net of enchantment, and everything had turned itself inside-out. Dogs ruled the world. Hot was cold. Peacock feathers were sprouting out of everyone's forehead.

Whatever I had seen and felt, it was an omen of good fortune. Shaula Pearl was tagged by light, as divine as it gets. It left me with a feeling - the path less trodden, the hidden path, was our journey, hand in hand. Hand in paw. It was dark nights and howling banshees, but it was speckled with starlight and a glow dog and the silken wings of love, flickering softly, charming the most despairing soul.

This magical morning was Piglet, all the way. "Sometimes the smallest things take the most room in your heart." How brilliantly said. I agree with that, feeling joy in the simple things. It isn't my new fence. It's a patch of wild strawberries, in a corner of the yard. It isn't a newly designed bathroom. It's the five inch rainbow on the wall, coloring a toddlers hand.

Small reminders, from the spirit world, are sometimes the most potent. Once, I bought an old convertible that was in dire need of enchantment. I was taking it through a car wash when the back material ripped open, and a flood of water hit the back of my head. As I drove home, wet and cold, I looked up and said, "Okay, God. Anything else?" My rear view mirror fell in my lap. I laughed. It was a better option than screaming. You can't be angry if you're making fun of a situation.

Five years later, the need for a sense of humor, lingers strongly, reminding me that enchantment has side-effects, always needing to be embraced. I was visiting Rachael, one night, and came home with a plate of warm cookies. Shaula Pearl had a surprise for me, also. Large chunks of foam were scattered all over my bedroom. Her dog bed was gutted. I ate two cookies, immediately. There is madness behind the foam. She refuses to go out the front door, so walks are out. A dog has to burn off energy.

Shaula Pearl and I ended our first week together without battle scars and with a growing respect for the unknown. With the charming intervention of Divine Light, I was flying on the wings of hope, impatient as ever. I wanted to birth her into the future where third eyes were illuminated daily and where she glowed in the daylight, as bright as she did under the moon. Instead, I went shopping at a local pet store, buying a large dog gate, securing it at the entrance of the kitchen. I was hoping to give her a change of scenery when I returned to work. Besides, it was roomy like a play pen. She could explore and sniff things. I left her alone in the kitchen, for a short time on Sunday, telling her that she was a gated community of one, sometimes two, if I joined her. I hyped it up. "You are so privileged! People pay big time to live behind a gate!" She didn't buy into it. She sat on the floor, sighing loudly.

On Monday, before I left for work, I added to her elite kitchen, a few biscuits, a paper bag, a pair of old fluffy socks, and a stuffed buffalo, hoping she would entertain herself. Despite her more pleasant environment, I felt sick most of the day, worrying about how she was doing. My unruly imagination haunted me. Maybe she had turned on the water faucet and was swimming. When I got home, it was a jaw-dropper, but at least, not an emergency. She was sitting on top of the oven, looking more like a mountain goat than a dog. To Shaula Pearl, it was a place sturdy enough to hold her weight. I couldn't get her to come down, so I washed my hair, wondering during the rinse stage, if she was comfortable. As with anything new and abnormal, you have to shift your perspective. An oven can snag a tail.

To my relief, the week went smoothly, in the sense of nothing happening, outside of the ordinary oddness, except for one night. It was raining hard for Ventura County, which means you could hear it. Around nine pm, the electricity went off, at the exact moment when Shaula Pearl blasted into the backyard, banging through the doggie door. I have no idea what frightened her. The lights came back on, as I belly walked her into the dining room. A moment later, they went out.

My house was ink black. She squirmed out of my grasp. I couldn't see her, but I could heard her. She was running all over the downstairs, bumping into things, knocking over a water bottle on the table and skidding across the kitchen floor, dumping over a trash bag. The lights went on for a few seconds. Miraculously, she was by the stairs. I walked over to her quickly, throwing my arms around her middle, as my clock radio went on with a blast of white noise. The lights went out again. We belly walked up the stairs. I released her in the hallway, knowing that she could maneuver in the dark, better than I could. She flew into her crate like her paws were on fire.

I didn't feel like writing, worried about her, so I lit a chocolate scented candle and sat by her on the carpet, reading a book about the angelic meaning of number sequences. I looked at my phone. It read 4:44. Angels are surrounding you. They know what you need. Don't worry. You have help. I recited the message to Shaula Pearl, who looked calmer that I expected. She also had a message for me. "I'm okay." That was it. Simple and direct, the way of dogs. I was humbled. I needed to have more faith in her. Shaula Pearl seemed less of a mess than I was. Considering everything, I felt optimistic. I couldn't imagine another night as strange as this one. What was I thinking?

After a week of no visitors, it was time to introduce her to Rachael. As she entered the house, Shaula Pearl was sitting in her crate with her paws crossed. My royal chocolate was there, guiding her in the ways of goddess posture. It made me grin. I gave Rachael only a few suggestions. Walk in quietly. Be yourself. No intense energy. Here's how it went.

"Hi mom. Where is she?"

"Talk softer. She's in her crate in the dining room."

"She's so beautiful. I love the peacock thing on her head. Hi Shaula Pearl."

"Sit on the rug, in front of her. Don't look her in the eyes.

"Okay. Where should I look?"

"Look at her paws and talk to her."

"Shaula Pearl. You are so pretty."

"Snuff. Grunt. Puff."

"Mom. What is she doing?"

"Making noises. I'll know what she means eventually."

"She sounds scared."

"She is, but at least she's saying something."

That was enough chatting for Shaula Pearl, who had inched backwards, as far as she could, with her 'Do you eat dog' look. Rachael looked at me with concern but nodded her head and then hugged me. She knew what I was up to. She understood the word magic. It has nothing to do with pink-eyed rabbits popping out of a hat. Magic is snow, wearing a red cardinal. A peach glazed sky. The creamy white arms of the moon, embracing the night. The soul of a dog.

The weekend was welcomed. It was non-spooky. It also threw me onto another path, with Shaula Pearl in full agreement. I received a phone call from Nellie, a relatively new friend of mine who supported my passion for animals and chocolate. She rescues turtles, and claims an obsession with brownies. We talked mostly about animals and how much they add to the world. At the end of our conversation, she said, "I would love to meet your dog. Write a happy ending." Lightbulb! The idea of writing a book about Shaula Pearl, hadn't occurred to me, which was strange in itself. It grew roots immediately. The title poured into my head like a flash flood. It felt right. It made everything seem more enchanting, because now, it was a journey to share.

Your life can reinvent itself on the spin of a dime, whether it's a commitment to ignore chocolate, which doesn't make any sense, get a cat for the first time, or in my case, to adopt a six year old rescue dog with special needs. In her case, it wasn't a physical disability or a genetic disorder. It was a defect in a human. From what I understand, hoarding is an illness. It involves a total lack of awareness concerning the harm that you are causing your animals. Basic needs are often overlooked such as food, water, shelter, and medical aid. In the worst cases, you add in the abuse. Three thousand cases of hoarding animals are reported each year which adds up to 250,000 animals in horrific conditions. These are only the ones reported, and most often, by a neighbor or someone who knows the hoarder.

The description of hoarding is lacking. It should include the cruel and vicious crushing of beautiful souls. Preventative measures should be in place. There should be Soul 101 classes offered on college campuses, raising an awareness of the soul and how to help soul disorders such as hoarding and abuse. We should raise our children to be aware of the spirit world as much as the electronic world. Love and joy should be talked about at the dinner table, along with, "Have you started your homework?" Life should be about raising love energy. Plugging into joy. Talking about hope and healing and asking each other daily, "Did you say or do anything today that made a soul feel enchanted?"

CHAPTER SEVEN

LUSH LANDSCAPES OF GRACE

*"Dismiss all that insults your soul.
Cling to the truth and beauty
that feeds your passions."*
Walt Whitman

Love. Deep, rich and poetic. The flesh of our souls.
Hope. The feet of our dreams, running with them.
Faith. The wing of a bird, searching for the sky.
Grace. The silence of snow falling. The unfolding of a rose.
The space between the beats of your heart.

The second month was greeted with a good dose of truth serum. There was a loud knock at the door, late in the evening. I hate that. If you live alone, and your mind has uncontrollable thoughts, an inherited trait, there could be a Cyclops on your welcome mat, munching on a coyote, explaining the lack of sightings in the neighborhood. I was fortunate. I wasn't yet adept at making my thoughts manifest instantly. It was a friend from out-of-state, surprising me with a visit. She sat on my couch carefully, as if it might bite her. "What's different?" she inquired, looking around the room. "I don't really care," she added quickly, hugging me. "I miss you. Don't you have a new dog? A rescue dog? That's what I heard."

"I do," I replied eagerly, always passionate about those I love. "I live with the amazing wonder dog, Shaula Pearl." I pointed upstairs. "She won't come down. She's too modest about all the work she's done, remodeling the house." I started to laugh. Thankfully, my friend did, also. After a short time, I escorted her to her car, noticing the night sky and the splash of stars sprinkled across the heavens like celestial glitter. The simple elegance of light, the face of God, always wanting us to observe more than ourselves.

Craving dessert, but too tired to hunt down ingredients, I made tea, with a shameless amount of honey, and folded up into my tie-dye bean bag, noticing a tear in it. Behind me, my expensive saffron blinds, next to my rent-to-own couch, were twisted and bitten. I was tired of them anyways. I looked at my large arm chair, gutted at the bottom, trying to remember what it felt like to sit in it. The two enormous throw rugs, covering most of the downstairs carpet, added a leopard look. Maybe my décor was jungle? I moved to the kitchen. It was missing a napkin holder and a bread box. My friend was right, of course. My house was different. My dog was different. Extraordinarily different.

I was suffering from selective blindness. I knew what the downstairs looked like, but I didn't really see it, like Mesa's muzzle. I thought of a conversation at a staff meeting. Hair color became an intense topic. I declared with zealous passion, "I will never go any shades of gray!" I thought it was a lovely color, but not on my head. The lady across from me, stated the same thing, but her hair was two-thirds gray. I'm not telling her, and it doesn't matter. However you see things, rights your world.

What truly astounds me, is that I still have company over, or better said, they still want to come over. I'm grateful, but I need at least a twenty-four hour notice to make the house semi-presentable. I light at least four large scented candles, wash all the area rugs, burn incense, put out a normal display of objects, and scent the house with food items in my cupboard, minutes before anyone arrives. Microwave popcorn is a great scent, along with freshly baked brownies. If I'm feeling creative, I make a homemade potpourri, The Shaula Pearl Brew. A large pot, filled with half water and half apple cider, provides your base. Add chunks of apples and oranges. Throw in cinnamon and allspice and be generous. Boil and simmer. It scents the entire house. If you think you can spare any, throw in some chocolate chips. Throw in flower petals. Do whatever makes you feel happy. Do everything happy.

Shaula Pearl had the run of the house now. Also, I wired her crate door open. I wanted her to feel free and limitless in her choices. It made for some weird routines. When it was time for dinner, she wasn't on a leash anymore, sitting by me. That was normal and so was the fact that she was listening, like any other dog. She would hear me, opening the cupboard door and then hunting for the can opener that I can never locate. She would come down the stairs but only half way. The problem was, I hadn't mastered the art of disappearing. If I approached her, carrying her food bowl, she would bolt to her closet. If I fed her, inside her closet, she would knock the bowl over. I tried going outside, but for some reason, it made her nervous, and she wouldn't eat. I would end up, putting her food bowl in her crate. When that happened, she would eat. I wanted to eliminate crate time, so I kept searching for an eating experience that worked for her. Finally, one morning, I hid in the downstairs closet, placing her food bowl on the rug. I'm not sure why, but she liked that, except once. It was my fault. I tripped on a candle, falling out of the closet and into her water bowl. She wouldn't eat until evening.

Her eating habits made sense. Food, coupled with myself, was a new experience, not to be trusted, especially now that she was off a leash, at least inside the house. She didn't have to sit with me. She could do what she wanted, but she needed to eat. Children can also have food issues, if they come from abused backgrounds. Tasting new food can be frightening. Their comfort zone doesn't include much. Shaula Pearl seemed to exhibited similar traits. Crispy chicken, hotdogs, sausage, all of the normal mouth-watering food items, were sniffed at and ignored. Also, hoarding is common in neglected children, hiding things in their cubbies or secret places. It makes sense. Things can fill you up with a fake sense of power and control. Once, I found a large pile of trash in a child's back pack, full of dried up bottles of paint, broken pencils, and wadded up paper from a trashcan, plus flowers from the playground. At the bottom of all this, was a deflated football.

Shaula Pearl was beginning to hoard. First, it was food. She would hunt for anything edible, all over the house, only to hide it. Once, I came home from work, and there were paw prints on top of the oven. The bag of bagels was missing from the top of the refrigerator. I found two of them in her closet. Also, the mystery of where your other sock goes, somewhere inside the secret universe of the dryer, was apparent in my household. It was Shaula Pearl. She collected my socks, making a pile of them in her bedroom. Once, I found all of her stuffed animals, that she never played with, under her bed.

Her odd behavior was logical, not only from her abuse issues, but she had never been told that anything was inappropriate. She would lie on almost any surface that was large and flat enough to support her weight. After work, she could be anywhere in the house, but she favored high elevation such as the dining room table and the kitchen counter. As usual, it was impossible to move her. My best tactic was to join her. Instantly, she would jump off.

Toward the middle of the second month, she mastered a fear. She ate in front of me, but she would stretch out like a long rubber band, ready to run. Also, she was developing little quirks. Sometimes, she wouldn't eat out of her bowl, but she would eat off a dinner plate – good goddess potential, doing what feels right.

It's funny what you don't miss when you don't have it. I didn't miss my less worrisome life of living with dogs who were naturally enchanted. I didn't miss the lightbulbs at night. I didn't miss the doorbell. I'm sure that I was on the neighborhood's mysterious person list with a footnote - held captive by a large animal with a scary neck. Also, If you came over, you would have to speak softly and move slowly. A few good souls would brave the entrance hall, but when they did, Shaula Pearl would pound down the hallway, hiding in her closet. It would confirm suspicions that strange things were happening here, and it was best to ignore them.

The trick was, never to meet and greet Shaula Pearl on the stairs. My youngest daughter Wendi, came home for a visit and experienced this, first hand. I was out shopping when she called me with a reasonable comment. "Mom. Your dog's scaring me. She's on the stairs, and I can't get past her. She's making strange sounds."

"What kind of sounds," I asked, already guessing.

"Kind of a heavy breathing. Puffing. Gurgling," she answered, sounding a little nervous herself.

"Gurgling might be intense snuffing," I said, getting no response. I added, "Okay. Just back up. Stay calm. I'm coming right home after I buy the brownie mix." She appreciated that more, after dinner.

I was positive, the backyard would become an enchanting place, because it was outside. Just like children, dogs need to put their paws in grass and feel connected to the earth, not detached from it. Being messy, and running until you're out of breath, is enchanting. Physical activity urges the release of happy hormones into your body and pumps you up with oxygen, a good stress reliever.

Feeling strongly that it was in her best interest, I unleashed her in the backyard for the first time. She paced from one end of the yard to the other, non-stop. "You're feeling happy!" I yelled, trying to convince her. At least, she was getting some exercise. I sat in the grass, watching her and thinking about the Houdini Chihuahua who had escaped a yard. I kept an eye on her. We did this often, pacing and sitting in the grass together. The downside was, outside noises were scary. The sudden caw of a crow or even a strong breeze, would send her running inside. Once, she ran inside from the loud coo of a dove, but stopped for second, sniffing the top of a weed, flowering up out of a cement crack on the patio. That was grace.

Sounds are challenging, no matter who you are. They never leave us. They stalk us. For that reason, we also become insensitive to them. I did an experiment once with a group of college students, focusing on sound. I gave them a choice, both teemed unfair. They had to give up their car radio for a week or their CD's. Moans. Gulps for air. It was a worse reaction than a surprise quiz. At the end of the week, I had a varied amount of responses. Some of the students felt anxious. Others admitted, they felt calm and didn't have any meltdowns. Amazingly, a small group of students confessed, the radio now assaulted their hearing. The brain revels in its plasticity, able to adapt to new situations, rewiring our thinking. When I gave up regular soda, to befriend diet soda, there was no turning back. My old friend was too sweet and syrupy. Even so, I felt like a traitor, giving up on a loyal companion I had swallowed for years.

One night, we were both assaulted by sound. My cell phone was hiding from me, taunting me with my incoming lyric, Mustang Sally. I was ready to scale a fence. Shaula Pearl was freaking out, running all over the upstairs, trying to escape the noise. I couldn't pinpoint it. When you don't hear in one ear, everything sounds deceiving. Five minutes later, I found it in her crate under a blanket. It was the first time that I discovered anything in her crate. Lesson learned. Never assume, because it hasn't happened, it won't happen. I felt compelled to call Julia. The first thing she said was, "There's a noise in your house that goes off and on. Shaula Pearl doesn't like it. It's too loud, but it has a good beat." It's too loud because I can't hear it, otherwise. I compromised. Mustang Sally was retired to loud chimes.

I assumed the following day would be calmer with Sally's retirement. I was wrong. A new challenge arose, one that I had been warned about. I came home from work, and the entire downstairs had a new décor - tornado. Shaula Pearl had her first panic attack. A lamp was knocked over and so was the large vase sitting on the floor. The fake pussy willows were now on the dining table, half chewed. The throw pillows, on the couch, were now on the stairs. Area rugs were crumpled up in piles. The kitchen wasn't much better. My pot holders and small towels were on the floor, along with some candles and bills, previously on my desk.

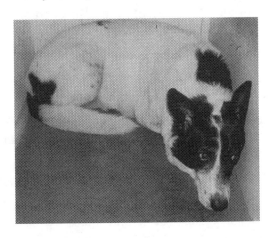

I found her in her closet. It was a good time for a heart to heart chat. I told her about my job and how important it was that I showed up, at least physically. I promised her that I would always return. We were family, and I would never leave her. I listened to her response. She snuffed and gurgled. She puffed once, pretending to ignore me, but she was listening. She told me that she worried about being alone. I told her again that I would always come home, that my socks and my toaster were here, and my laptop. Most importantly, she was here, and she was the heart of the house, as far as I was concerned.

Later that night, I felt her so much, it startled me. Why? Perhaps without knowing it, I had become partially immune to my own well of feelings. Connecting to each other, spirit-to-spirit, is a natural state and so easily forgotten. We should feel and sense everything in the world, all of its colors and moods. We should feel the sky with our hands, a cold, blue lapis, smooth and polished, and the lavender robe of dusk, soft and supple, lined with black swan feathers. We should feel the sunlight, torching the leaves of a red maple in rich, violet reds, glowing like garnets set in wood.

Toward the end of the month, Shaula Pearl was untethered and unpredictable, but that was a good thing. It made for a good match. We had things in common. Besides that, she didn't pace anymore, inside the house, but she did pace in the backyard. Happy hormones were flying. I remained optimistic on her mental state, plus on locating the perfect place to dismiss food items. I tried to be helpful. "Hey. I found some options," I would yell, as she zoomed by. "Behind the palm tree. In the ditch. In the gopher hole." She did manage to find a few spots at the end of the yard, but she also found some in front of the doggie door, inside the house. I called my friend Cassie, a veterinary assistant who was studying to be an animal doctor. I asked her why Shaula Pearl didn't relieve herself outside, all of the time. Her answer made sense. To squat, puts you in a vulnerable position. If you needed to, you couldn't bolt as quickly. She was evidently feeling more comfortable inside the walls of the house. I was happy that she was feeling safe, but it was a slow death sentence for the carpet.

In spite of some non-enchanted areas, Shaula Pearl was beginning to feel the initial stages of enchantment. At night, when I was writing, she would sit in her crate with the door open, watching me. Off and on, she would belly crawl out of it, if only to run into her closet. She would always come back after a few minutes, plunging into her crate. An exception was about to happen. I was running on a writer's high, words pouring out like a faucet on full power. When that happens, there isn't much that can pull me out of it, except for the lure of baking cookies, or now, unusual sounds. I happened to hear one, glancing over my shoulder at Shaula Pearl, knocking my soda over with my elbow. My left hand caught it. I don't know how I managed to do that, except for the assistance of drink angels and perhaps Shaula Pearl angels. She was out of her crate, ears up and growling.

I was too shocked to say anything. Shaula Pearl, on the other hand, didn't feel that way. She began to bark and run around in circles. I stood up quickly, afraid that something in the house was dangerous. I followed her gaze, looking up at the ceiling over the bathroom door. I have a ledge there, that sticks out by at least a yard. Sitting as still and poised as an ebony statue, was a huge blackbird. Without thinking, I yelled, "I'm sorry! You have to leave!'

I was giving instructions to a wild bird, but the moment was so surreal. Shaula Pearl took it literally, barking until it flew off and then chasing it downstairs, feathers flying everywhere. The bird must have had exit angels, guiding it through the doggie door. I was glad but panicky for Shaula Pearl. If ever she had the momentum to scale a fence, it was now.

By the time I yanked open the glass doors, the bird was gone. What amazed me, even more than her barking, was the fact that she was outside and not pacing. She was panting and running around, looking for it. "Thank you," I said to the blackbird, "for finding your way into my bedroom." Shaula Pearl heard me. She froze, realizing that I was outside with her. I should have hidden in the ditch. She ran in, stumbling upstairs.

Anything she did felt miraculous, even a basic instinct to chase prey. Her canine ancestry had unleashed itself in full fury. I saw a magnificent, strong dog, rise up from her primordial roots, glowing. She looked focused, fearless, and in the moment. Even the earth, Mother Gaia, awakens a primal and powerful emotion in us, to live joyously and with abundance, not only with material pleasures, but with the richness of heart-inspired passions. I see it in Shaula Pearl, the way she reacts when she sniffs a flower or watches a lizard. She melts a little. Her head lowers. Her body droops and her tail swishes slowly, almost dreamlike. She slips into a safe place. Those are her doorways.

Enchantment was sprouting. I lit candles and burned sage, a tribute to the random happenings of life that make a difference. A bird in the bedroom was one of them, but it was more than it appeared to be, as most things are. The language of birds can be very cryptic.

This bird had a meaning, resonating with her enchantment. Like the crow, birds cloaked in black have a mysterious side. They don't give up their messages, directly. They want you to muse over them for a while, asking you to reach higher planes of thought. On a whole, they represent a transition in your life, away from a reality that wasn't working for you. If there was ever a Shaula Pearl-inspired message, blackbird brought it in.

I dreamed, a few nights later, that a very tall person, hidden in shadows, was giving me a message. I was told, in a soft but clear voice, that I would arrive where I wanted to be, a lot quicker, if I ran after my dreams instead of running away from my fears. My mother always told me to chase them. I would focus on that, encouraging Shaula Pearl to move forward, to focus on her strengths, and hopefully one day, walk out of her closet looking for me, or just looking - being in a world where she can do whatever she wants, without fears biting her legs.

During the third month, Shaula Pearl looked different, a little more poised and confident. Also, her walk changed. It was less robotic. Something was shifting in her, slowly, like the small increments of movement in a butterfly wing, warming itself up. She was more closet bound than crate bound. She was flowering, becoming more courageous and spirited. Also, she began to play. Glorious play, the raw joy of exploring. It was hers now but on her terms only. If I threw a ball or toy in her direction, she would run from it. Wiggling a stuffed dachshund in front of her seemed promising, at first. She would stare at it, and a moment later, back up. But when the house was dark, and I was in bed, then she would play.

It made sense. Night was magic to her. The house was quiet and dusky looking, and the world, gone. It didn't surprise me that she was less fearful in the dark. Our state of mind shifts, opening us up to our most guarded thoughts. The dark can glow, lighting our dreams, brightening our path with fairy lights, guiding us through the wild woods. It's a reflective time where fears are unveiled, giving us strength. Joy is the outcome. Joy is the child of enchantment who never grows old.

For Shaula Pearl, play began to warm up her joy. It was rumbling softly, under her glow fur, untethered now. Ebbing and receding, returning with bigger swells, sparkling and iridescent – the light of her soul, remember who she was, what shore she came from. Also, play came with her own definition. She poked things - her blankets, dust bunnies, a corner in the living room behind the chair. It was rummaging around, snuffing and pushing things over. It was a private affair. I had to be pretend that I didn't know she playing. If I caught her at it, she would stop. I learned the hard way, as usual. I heard a loud bang somewhere in the house. That wasn't so unusual, but it was followed by a thud. A thud is a deeper and more muffled bang. I decided I better investigate, just in case something truly abnormal was occurring. I peeked into the small bedroom, expecting to see her in the closet. She was there, but she was playing in it, plunging around with a sock and something else I couldn't quite see. She wiggled into a corner, exposing one of my favorite t-shirts, all balled up. I think she's magic. I don't know how she gets a hold of things. I gave her the t-shirt. It had so much hair on it, it would glow under the moon. She froze of course, seeing me. I backed up, leaving without a word, and mad at myself for disturbing a few moments of hard-earned joy.

I heard another thud, deep into the night. The web was spinning, catching her dormant dreams, trying to rouse them. The night grew slowly. Joyous intermissions kept me awake and curious. After a long pause, I sneaked into her room again, against my better judgement, crouching as low as I could without licking the carpet. This time, she wasn't aware of me. She was sleeping, curled up in a ball, eyes half opened. Joy can be exhausting. She found it among her pain. She went for it in a closet. I've learned from her. If it pleases me, I will spin in wild circles. I will sip honey out of a wooden bowl. I will grow wings of an owl and beat them to the rhythm of the night and see the world with bright moon eyes.

In the morning, I called Cassie, sharing her play session in the closet. She asked me to consider if she was having an anxiety attack. No way. I know her thud. She wasn't convinced, telling me that it was too soon to exhibit play behavior. She grilled me on the impossible event. Was her mouth open? Was her tongue floppy? Was her body stiff? Was she growling? I was beginning to gurgle. I knew my dog.

I adore my friend. I used to work with her at a preschool, spending a good part of our day making exuberant comments about goldfish and trying to keep earthworms safe. They can only stretch so far. Cassie meant well and is very knowledgeable, but you have to live a journey to truly understand it. Claim what you know.

My close friends were loyal to the enchantment plan, embracing my new lifestyle, still chocolate driven, which could explain it. They came knocking at the end of the month for a movie night. I clued them in to the new 'no screaming' law. An hour later, Shaula Pearl came down, peeking around the curve of the stairs. I didn't see her immediately, but my friend Belinda did, wagging her finger wildly, unable to say anything. We were all shocked. Shaula Pearl was in full gurgle and out of her closet. This was an enchanted milestone, a mile wide. She was curious. She wasn't afraid, but she was guarded.

Belinda said hi, putting her pizza down slowly, not sure what to expect. I looked at my friends who were stunned. I had a feeling, they were thinking, dog eats pizza. Dog eats people. I took the initiative, answering their silence. "She's okay. She won't bother anyone." I didn't think anyone knew what a significant moment this was for Shaula Pearl.

When the movie ended, I turned the lights on, cringing, knowing how the house looked under the stark glare of lightbulbs. My house was a disguised wreck, but you could sense the love in it. Belinda broke the silence, as usual. "Wow. I love your paper plates. Where'd you get them?"

Jennie added, "The pizza was great, and thanks for not having a side of anchovies."

Patsy sounded sincere. "When can we do it again? I really enjoy being here with everyone. We could do it at my house, but I have my dachshunds. They get a little possessive. Your house is really the best place. It's sets the mood." She lathered it on, but so did everyone, being my kind and gracious friends. My house, despite the candles, carried a scent of cinnamon and dog, and I could see one long strand of glow hair growing out of Belinda's toenail.

"Night everyone. Love you. Thanks for coming," I announced, pulling her to the door before she noticed it. I smiled. They smiled. Hugs of thank you went around twice, most likely, because it was my house that wasn't normal.

Three months of confronting your inner demon can be exhausting. After my friends left, Shaula Pearl retired to her closet, lying on her side. That was new. Up until tonight, she would sit in the closet, backed up against the wall, or she would rest on her belly, a better position to run. But even with her enchanting strides, the majority of things she did, were still fear-based. She ate like she was starving. She was anxious. She was curiosity. Stiff. Relaxed. Tense. Playful. She wanted to trust. She mistrusted most everything, but the realms of enchantment were descending, and she was feeling it.

During the night, there was a monstrous thud from the closet. A joy thud. Joy angels were pouring in. My heart melted. I realized how much I cared for her. I couldn't process a reality of never hearing a thud or looking at peacock fur. I focused on beautiful thoughts, flashing dots, glow dogs, and the sun inside of us, a shard of Divine Light, reminding us that we are all immortal souls, all dressed up, masquerading as mortals.

"We will never lose each other," I said, knowing that Shaula Pearl was listening. We will grow older together. Age is a lovely dream. Our skin becomes thin and beautiful, delicate like rice paper. Our hair grows pale and soft like flowers in the rain. Our mind is full of fragrant spices and the sweet scent of wild plums, and all the lovely moments of our life, a part of us now, giving us silver moon eyes and lips the color of golden wheat or the sea-washed pink of moon shaped pearls.

CHAPTER EIGHT

FRAGILE WEBS

"Take away love and our earth is a tomb".
Robert Browning

Four months in. Something in me shifted, this time. I wasn't anymore poised, still knocking over my soda, but I felt linked to Shaula Pearl, transcending all titles - dog owner, animal lover, chocolate fixated fool, who believes that your journey is more significant than the temporary demise of your home. To put it mildly, I was enchanted by a dog, love at first gurgle.

Love. It is a delicate and soft word on the exhale. It is everything we see and imagine. It is the flesh of angels. It is the deep emerald green of kale. It is the cool, damp earth, drinking rainwater, bursting open dark brown seeds, releasing the rainbow colored dreams of wildflowers. Love. We breathe it in. We breathe it out. It sustains us. It keeps us alive.

Shaula Pearl understands it. I see it in her eyes. If you doubt that animals love, in their wild hearts, look at death. You can't mourn or grieve without loving someone. Dolphins remain with a deceased infant or pod member for days. Chimpanzees will mope around by themselves in a zoo, refusing bananas, if there is a death among them. A baby elephant will shed tears and refuse to eat if his mother dies. Love is there when a baby elephant is born. The entire community gathers around it, making rumbling noises. Joyful noises.

More than anything, love is a healing balm. One night, while I was writing, Shaula Pearl seemed fidgety, moving from her crate to her closet and back to her crate again, about every ten minutes. She was quiet, but I always knew when she was traveling. Her energy is strong. After a while, I watched her more than I wrote, playing around with line spacing and indents. I was slumping in my chair anyways, too tired and blurry eyed to be inspired.

I opened a bag of chocolate covered pretzels for slumping emergencies, refusing to go to bed. I wrote for another hour, under the influence of sweet and salty. Shaula Pearl shifted her energy. It was more light-hearted, kind of bouncy. She half walked, half strutted down the hall to her bedroom, turned around like a runway model and came back to her crate. I didn't get it the first time. She did it again. Her paws were air-born, slightly bent at the ankles and with a spring to them. She was prancing. It was enchanted energy on the upsurge. You can't prance without feeling it. Fear was there, rattling around inside of her like a chest infection, but it was weakening, monthly.

The following morning, I had a hard time going to work, again. This time, I was suffering from the prance syndrome. I entered my office, feeling prance strong, when the lights went out, including phones and computers. I couldn't do any work, so I pretended to work, which meant, I was scribbling in my state regulations handbook designed for state funded early childhood centers. Without asking the state of California, I added a section titled, enchanted paws. I was grinning a mile wide, enjoying the power outage, when a co-worker walked into my office. I could tell she wanted to talk. Our conversation, not surprising, was dog oriented.

"Am I interrupting you? It looks like you're writing something."

"Nothing important," I said. "Just some foot notes."

"How's Shawna?"

"Shaula Pearl. She's good. How's Greta?"

"You won't believe what she did. She sat by the shower while I was washing my hair, howling the entire time. What do you think?"

"I think she wanted to come in with you."

"Maybe. She's so cute. She follows me everywhere."

"You're her person. She wants to be near you."

"Guess what else she did? She went to sleep on my pillow. I used an old one. I didn't want to wake her. Was that a little obsessive?"

"Maybe for some people. You and Greta have a special bond. It's all good. I had a dog who loved my pillow."

"What's Shaula done lately?"

"Shaula Pearl. She pranced. It's a big deal."

"Cool. Is she acting sociable? Affectionate?

"I think so. It's the way she looks at me. At first, it was a blank look. Now, it's more of a stare. She sees me. It's amazing."

"What do you mean by seeing you?" she asked, sitting down now.

I loved the question. "The mind sees more than the eyes," I replied, wondering what she was thinking about me. "For example, I changed my brand of peanut butter. When I looked in the refrigerator, I didn't see it. My mind was looking for the jar with the blue lid, not the red lid. Shaula Pearl's eyes work fine, but her mind didn't want to see me. She zoned me out in the beginning. It's a good escape mechanism."

"Back to work," she said, not very excited about the idea. I got that. Dogs were more inspiring than some of our work days. She had one more thing to say, as she left. "When I get home, I'm going to look at Greta, straight in her eyes, and tell her that she can have my pillow." I loved her comment. Eyes have plenty to say, not only from a spiritual aspect. I studied the eye when I was teaching a human development class. People have a variety of patterns in their Iris – lines, threads, curves, creating different shapes like eye art. The patterns are an indication of whether you are a warm and trusting person or more of a neurotic personality, giving into cravings. My iris would be the exception, no doubt. It would display a little of each.

I drove home that day, wondering if I was missing anything important that I wasn't seeing. It's easy to overlook the simple things that don't yell at you, like dust on the top of the refrigerator. I needed to quiet my mind, so I could hear better on a spiritual level. It's easy to live from the neck up where your brain is, firing off all those logical thoughts, disconnecting you from your body where your intuitive gut lives. My head and my heart needed to be working together.

I thought of Greta howling, reminding me of Mesa. When my house burned down, I had to leave her in the backyard for a few days, being with her as much as I could. At night, I would lean against the house, sleeping with her for hours. During the day, neighbors would see me in the driveway and run over, telling me that she was howling. In dog language, howling wasn't a fun thing unless you're a hound dog. Mesa was separated from her pack. She was mourning the loss of it.

Clearly, I'm not the perfect dog person. I make mistakes. Dog trainers would look at me, shake their book knowledge heads and tell me to get a video and a reality check. I admit, I'm intentionally clueless to the most effective training techniques. My dogs jump on me, tow me on a leash and trick me into thinking I know more. If I was on trial, my defense would be simple. I love my dogs. They are safe and joyful.

Shaula Pearl would be up for debate, no doubt. She pokes me with her nose, and I pet her. Poking a human is classified as an alpha trait. The first time she poked me in the side, her ears were back, a submissive trait. Also, I feed her first, something I've always done. An alpha dog eats first in the pack, but she was starving and anxious, so it seemed like an enchanted move. Treat your dog like an individual as you do your children. Taking into consideration what most professionals support, I raise alpha-submissive dogs with human tendencies. You won't find this in your basic dog book, but neither will you find a chapter on soulful, intentional affection.

All the strange and wonderful things that I have witnessed, sharing my life with dogs, leaves me convinced, they are truly magical creatures. I went to a psychic fair recently, where you pay ten dollars for ten minutes, sitting with as many readers as you can afford, or can't afford. I zeroed in on a pet psychic named Jessica. All she wanted me to do was write my dog's name on a scrap of paper. She looked at her name, with tears forming in her eyes. I became worried, wondering if Shaula Pearl was okay. Jessica apologized to me, explaining that she was overwhelmed with emotion. She couldn't believe how much my dog loved me. It was a shared emotion.

She continued to discuss Shaula Pearl in detail, touching on her loose bowel movements and her finicky eating. She advised me to lessen her food, that her insides were rebelling. She told me to massage her right hip gently. It was hurting her from arthritis. She took my hand after that, telling me that it was okay the way things were, that I wasn't insisting on certain established behaviors. My dog was different, and I was aware of it. She also mentioned that Shaula Pearl feared the sound of water. It was part of her abuse.

What struck me, as truly inspired, was everything. She was having some issues with her bowels. She bolts outside when I wash my hair, and she was beginning to favor her right side. I left the fair, reflecting on the fact that life can be so stunningly deceptive. If our spiritual abilities were functioning at their maximum level, we would see angels flying over our neighborhood and hear animals talking to us in pet stores. We would see uncle John, who passed away, sitting on our couch, reading a newspaper.

If you grew up in Ventura County, you might be inclined to believe that a thunder storm is a myth. The fourth month challenged the area legends. We got one with all the trappings of a dark and stormy night - sheet lightening, hard rain and boomers that could wake the dead. Friends were calling me. I called friends. We were all in shock. I figured it was a rogue storm, wanting some high adventure on the west coast. Being a storm lover, I bolted into the backyard, reveling in it. At the same time, I was concerned about Shaula Pearl and how she was dealing with it.

She came outside, minutes later, standing in the storm, quiet and composed. It occurred to me why she wasn't afraid. She had lived outside on the hoarder's ranch, located in the desert where storms were more prevalent. The natural sounds of nature were nonthreatening. They didn't hurt her. I looked at her, in awe of her secretive goddess powers. "Do you know how beautiful you are?" I asked her, admiring how she glowed, even during a dark storm. I wondered if I glowed?

I was enthralled with glow. I forgot the rules. Shaula Pearl was in charge of her own enchantment. I approached her cautiously, with my hand extended, attempting to pet her. She scuttled back a few feet, turning her head sideways, giving me her one eyed look. She ran into the house after that, leaving me soaked and guilt-ridden. She wasn't ready to be touched yet, at least, a personal touch.

I should have known better. I was still an object of great curiosity and uncertainty. Furthermore, she had a collection of little quirks, spotlighted around me. When I changed into my pajamas, she would bolt. If I looked different, dying my hair or wearing a new bathrobe, she would look at me like I had two heads. Also, doors were freaky to her. She didn't like them opened, mainly closet or bathroom doors. When I thought about it, it made sense. She would see me, and seconds later, I would vanish into a small, dark room, or I would communicate with a strange looking object that made weird, gurgling noises. Even now, she doesn't like a drawer sticking out of my dresser or a gift bag on the floor. It's different, so it's dangerous.

We had a great evening routine going. Dinner. Music. Candles. Incense. Chocolate. Writing. Chocolate. Writing. I could chant that to a drum beat. When it was time for bed, and the lights dimmed, Shaula Pearl would disappear into her closet. A few minutes later, she would explore the house. Sometimes, I would hear a rattling sound. It was her body, barreling through the doggie door. Transitions were still a challenge for her. If she was upstairs, I would hear more of a soft thump. She was rummaging around in her closet, her own ritual. It made me smile. How much can you do in a small closet? Evidently, there was plenty.

She woke up early one morning, at four. I have a mother's ear. I woke up with her, hearing her shuffling something around. A few loud clanking sounds followed. I wondered if she had gotten into the trash bag in the kitchen. She pounded upstairs, shortly after, thudding into her closet. The mystery clank would keep me awake. I grabbed my camera on the way down, out of habit. The trash was upright, but there was an empty dog food can on the floor and one on my desk. She's funny. Back upstairs to think on my abnormal blessings.

I was side-tracked, half way up. Shaula Pearl was in her room, looking at me. The body-less dog. All I could see was her head. I can fairly say, it was her peeking stage. She peeked around corners, behind chairs and over objects. Sometimes, I didn't see her, she was so well camouflaged. It melted my heart. There was a hunger behind it. She wanted to feel safe. She wanted to believe that I was safe. She also wanted to feel accepted, just the way she was. I felt that very strongly. Pooh was feeling it. "The things that make me different, are the things that make me."

I did meditate after that, mentally talking to her. I told her that all souls are different. How boring if we all had lavender hair, wore jeans and t-shirts and drove black cars with purple tinted windows. My world would be good. I also told her that she looked like a dog on the outside. On the inside was the realm of the real Shaula Pearl, who was dog, but was a cosmic fusion of untethered joy and ribbons of bright light, swirling through the night sky with her soul on fire, the moon in her eyes and the sun in her belly. Her soul was a part of everything, and at the same time, it was unique and exceptional.

Later that day, I was in the kitchen inhaling cookie dough. I was feeling a little anxious, not sure why. I inhaled deeper, but it didn't stall my uneasiness. I assumed it was the evening festivities, a party at a friend's house. I'd be out late. I wrapped up the cookies, minus one, and spent the afternoon, writing and talking to Shaula Pearl, who was traveling between her closet and the crate without much of a prance. I wondered if she was feeling what I was feeling, as nondescript as it was. Meanwhile, my gut was twisting like a pretzel.

The day came and went quickly without any unfamiliar oddness, but I couldn't shake the idea that something was brewing, far from tasty. When it was time to leave, I put a shoebox in the living room, adding a few small biscuits and then putting the lid on. A little search and seizure might be fun. I walked out, got in the car, turned on the engine and turned it off. My gut had more than a few butterflies in it. There was a whole migration of them fluttering their wings. I felt queasy, leaving the car and unlocking the front door.

The house was quiet like a tomb. I walked in, shivering. A shriek pierced the air. I bolted upstairs, afraid that Shaula Pearl was in danger or an intruder was in the house, and she was defending her closet. Thank goodness, I didn't have to search and seizure, but it was the only thing good about it. I found her, curled up between the bathtub and the toilet. With the door open now, she ran to her closet where she stayed the remainder of the night. I was upset at myself beyond words. I had shut the door, but evidently, not tight enough. Her body must have pressed against it, closing it.

I placed a large dog cookie, near one of her paws, with a dollop of peanut butter on it. It was a gesture of good faith that I would make every effort to be non-human and quit making mistakes. I did leave for a while, after that, delivering the cookies, but came home shortly after, thankful that our bodies work with our souls, sending us messages. I sat with her for a while and wrote her a short apology.... Hungry snapdragons. Too hungry to notice. Too much in a hurry. The garden was gone. They ate each other except for one. She stood tall in her pastel petals snapping at the sun.

Shaula Pearl forgave me. She had eaten my token of apology. It was her way of saying, "I forgive you. I will eat your cookie." She left her closet about an hour later, settling into her crate. One day, she will stare at me with cookie eyes, and I will make every cookie recipe in my cookbook. Animals seek after what makes them feel good, just like humans. When I was a teenager, my iguana knew what he wanted. Once a week, I would place a variety of flowers in his cage from my mother's garden. He always went for the morning glories, aware of their hallucinogenic properties. He intentionally preferred to feel joyful.

Shaula Pearl was thawing on defrost mode. Her stiffness was still obvious, but it was melting monthly. It was amazing to witness, despite the fact that I was still dodging land mines on the carpet and the occasional foam. Credit is due. Divine Light, the energy of immeasurable love, plus the mood enhancers of chocolate, will always support us both. Shaula Pearl was open to it. She never gave up, growing wings and fairy paws. Also, she looked different from every angle. Her neck was less stiff. Her body moved and breathed. Her eyes weren't darting around or popping out of her skin. She didn't tilt as much.

One evening, I entered the house expecting whatever the universe had submitted. I looked up as usual, and there she was, standing calmly in the hallway, balanced and upright, with her tail up. It was twitching at the tip. Enchantment had tagged her tail. In my head, that was a wag. The rational side of my brain was telling me that I imagined it – a large moth, fluttering in the hallway. A tail fantasy after a long work day. No. I saw it move. I stared at her tail, a good part of the night, willing it to wag. Nothing. I went to bed, wondering if my left brain, my logical brain, was indeed, shrunken and emaciated from years of ignoring it. If that was the case, all logic was close to vanishing. I grabbed my cell phone and called Julia. " "Hey friend," I said, feeling a little idiotic. "I know this isn't a mind altering, spiritual experience, but I had this tail wagging vision." I told her what I saw. Her answer was in true Julia fashion.

She explained to me, "When you see something you aren't expecting, it's a gift. Trust the inner you, your spirit. It lives in a different dimension in your body. It's always trying to show you everything. You were supposed to see it, and you did."

I grunted, playing into it. "Why can't you just say, you saw her tail wag. Trust yourself."

"I did," she said, laughing at me.

I hung up, happy. My right brain, oozing with intuitive neurons, won. It was a wag.

I called Cassie the next day, wanting some information on the dog tail. She was very animated, stating that tail-wagging is similar to a human smile. Also, she told me that Shaula Pearl would never wag her tail, to anything inanimate, if she was alone, even her food bowl. Tails are socially responsive, connected to the brain. It made sense, since the brain powers the entire body.

"Think of it this way," she said, eager to explain further. "Do you ever smile at something that can't respond?" I told her no. I restated my answer, admitting that I smiled at chocolate and cookies.

I was close to saying goodbye when her inner psychiatrist emerged. She asked me a few questions. "Did she wag it high in the air? That could mean aggression. Was her tail rigid? That could mean a warning. Was her tail only half raised? She might be feeling anti-social."

I reminded her that it was only the tip of the tail that wagged. "Not much information on the tip," she answered, good-heartedly. I didn't care. Tail angels were present. She claimed her name. Her tail was a Shaula tail, a glow tail, a star on the rise.

'Happy' laps over. I woke up, the following morning, to a muffled thud. What I saw, didn't make any sense. Again, enchantment was pouring in from the spiritual realms in lavish amounts. Shaula Pearl was lying in her dog bed. I was stunned also, at her position. She looked as limp as a rag doll. I thought of Wicca, who slept in full joy, always running after something, twitching her legs and grunting softly with little snorts. Mesa was the queen of sleep, oblivious to her surroundings. She would sleep on the couch or on a face towel, as long as it had some semblance of comfort. Shaula Pearl had her own style going. The goddess flop. There must be magic in a dog bed.

I had breakfast with a group of teachers whom I had worked with at a previous job. Rosabella showed up with a picture of her new dog, who looked giddy like he had won the world. He had, in his own way, winning his forever human. Rosabella looked giddy, too. I looked non-giddy. Moods can hit for even irrational reasons. She noticed my droopy face. I told her that it had nothing to do with her apricot poodle who looked cute enough to put in a pie. It came out wrong. She giggled, crunching up her face, squishing her nose, and kissing her photo. I knew the body language. No one's cuter than my dog.

I hadn't meant to, but I sighed, loud and miserable sounding. "Are you okay?" she asked me, petting her photo.

"Kind of," I said, grabbing the dessert menu, needing support. "I was just thinking about my dog. I'll explain in a minute."

It was critical decision time. Most of us opted for the mile high chocolate cake. I demonstrated the art of delicately pricking it with a dessert fork, releasing all calories. Everyone participated but Bert, who smiled compassionately at me before eating a mile-high bite.

"Look everyone," I said, swallowing without fear. "I've been feeling a little in a funk lately. I want to know something impossible - what Shaula Pearl looked like as a puppy. It won't change anything. Why am I so obsessed with this? It doesn't make any sense."

Bert offered an insightful response, which I admitted to. "Things don't have to make sense. Anyways, you might be an obsessive person." Rosabella smirked, obviously knowing me. "Let me redeem myself," Bert continued. "You rescued her. You're curious. You want to know everything about her, because you care about her. It won't fix her, but you would feel good in some kind of a weird, imaginary way. Didn't mean to say weird. How does that sound?"

"No. I like the word weird," I answered, knowing how weird and wonderful my life was.

Bert got applause. He beamed as wide as the cake. He was right, of course. If I had a picture of her, nothing would change. In my head, it's a human need to know, so you gather information about what you don't know. I went home and hit the computer. I googled border collie mix, looking at pictures of puppies for at least an hour. Bert was right about obsessions. On some obscure level, I felt better. I was convinced, she was part shepherd and blue healer. I can only hope that she was treated with kindness when she was young. If not, it was affecting her negatively, the same as her abuse. Speaking harshly to a baby or a young child, weakens brain cell connections and can have life-long damaging effects. To cover all bases, I would beef up the joy meter.

A few years ago, I had practice. I substituted in a small class, consisting of four year olds with severe mental and physical challenges. One little boy had a misshapen head, fragile looking and pointed. He looked at me with the most beautiful set of eyes. They were sapphire blue and large as nickels. The assistant teacher left, shortly after I arrived, on a ten minute break. The children, who were sitting at a large table, were basically doing nothing. Children are children. They need to move and jiggle and feel joyously silly. Besides, movement is the way children learn. I made a quick search of the room and found a recorder and an old Elvis Presley tape. We rock and rolled. The mood in the room shifted dramatically. Blank expressions became little smiles. Motionless bodies became wiggly. Within a minute, nobody was sitting. Joy claimed the moment.

This very pleasant memory gave me ideas. I would hide biscuits in almost empty peanut butter jars. I would throw old rolls of wrapping paper on the rug. I would put tissue paper in the living room, all crunched up, with treats hidden among the folds. I would howl to the night sky and offer the moon a plate of marshmallows, if I thought it would push joy buttons.

It was a month of magical tails and goddess sleep positions, but I broke a promise. I came home from work, looking up as usual, scanning the hallway for a dog shape. I couldn't see her. The bathroom door was shut, but I stopped trusting the normal. I opened it, more out of paranoia. She wasn't there. My worst fear was shouting the word escape. She would be lost, again. I would go crazy and eat morning glories forever. That would be nonproductive, so I had to find her. I walked throughout the house, calling her name. The only reason why I remained sane, was because of my gut. It was trying to tell me that she was safe, and I should calm down. I clung to that, trampling through the wild woods in the yard. She was nowhere.

It finally occurred to me that I hadn't checked the garage. The door in the kitchen was open by an inch. I peeked in, fearful of the inevitable. I would find her but in what condition. She was nowhere to be seen, at first. I took a slow step in, listening. Silence pervaded the garage for a couple of long seconds. It was soon shattered with a loud scraping sound, coming from the end of the garage, right before the trashcan fell over. She came bolting out in the open, freezing the moment she saw me. We belly walked into the kitchen. I felt like mud.

Mud made me write. I needed the support of words, feeling beyond apologetic. Writing grew roots with me years ago. When I was twelve, I would sneak out of the house at night and climb my dream tree. I would write for hours, balancing on a thick branch. I was always aware of the moon, watching me between leaves. It was there, I wrote my life.

Shaula Pearl was in her closet for most of the evening. I sat by her, writing and reading to her. These are the bonding memories I will always remember, more than anything....The wild hare, walking the path of his soul. He has no dreams of being a wolf or large bear or an owl, following a hare's shadow. He makes merriment with the magic in his own life. That is enough for him, crunching and popping twigs, as he bounds and leaps. He wonders at the mist in the morning as dew forms, dressing the grass and dripping languorously off plants. He sips from creek water, sparkling in sun glitter. Later in the day, he wears moon spun shawls, draped over dusty blue primroses and the rosy purples of wood asters. He hops softly on the quiet fabric of moss and patches of tiny flowers, knitted together. He is content with his world for it is rich and luxurious. He lacks for nothing."

CHAPTER NINE

DIVINELY WIRED FOR JOY

"You can live as if nothing is a miracle.
You can live as if everything is a miracle."
Albert Einstein

The fifth month was full of surprising revelations, making me a life-time follower of magic. Soul magic. It parties with the soul of nature - the ancient songs of the rain, soft and rhythmic, humming them on your roof or tapping them out on large leaves. The brilliance of an orange canna leaf soaked in sunlight. The chalk white bark of a birch tree standing ghost-quiet at nightfall.

When you align your soul with the physical world, you have it all – natural magic. You feel alert and alive. Every moment becomes a doorway to your dreams, to other realms, to your creative muses. You are mindful of your body breathing, of dust spiraling in a sunbeam, of raindrops hitting a puddle, creating little concentric circles. You feel an exhilaration for the day. You stand firm, wearing the sky as a hood, the earth on your feet and the succulent perfumes of dawn on your skin. A gray rock, smooth and cool, slumbering in soil, dreaming of being a rock, shares his humor. He is a godfather of the earth, existing in the fullness of his own potential. That is magical living. It leaves me drunk on joy.

Thank you, Shaula Pearl.

When you are injured mentally, healing takes place in a nonphysical location – your mind. It's a harder scenario than a broken limb. You can't schedule an operation. You can't even find the mind.

The full potential of it is so sprawling, so vast, that it travels the universe, riding on the back of the soul.

Healing, in Shaula Pearl, would take place in her memories housed in her brain. I could work with that. I looked at her from my chair, with the hallway between us. She was lying on her own bed with the buffalo by her side. She was healing. Her thoughts were less frightening. Her room was helping. It was a physical place, small and safe like a burrow of a rabbit.

My own burrow was looking pretty sockless, along with constant smudgy areas on walls, thud inspired. Also, there was a rip in my comforter. My bedroom needed a facelift, as much as the downstairs, but it held my dreams, coiled in computer wires, and it held Shaula Pearl. I ignored what didn't support me. I was well aware of the spider web, thrashed by a wild wind. One thread left, but it cradles the entire design. That is the thread you hold onto. That is faith.

One particular night was a ghost night, full of fog and mist. I love to set moods. I darkened the entire house, lit purple candles and burned rosemary incense. After that, I wrote. A few hours slipped by easily. Shaula Pearl was on her bed, resting quietly, with her buffalo under her chin. I needed a break, so I loped into the kitchen, high on fantasy, and grabbed a soda, vowing that I would sleep at some point. I wrote for a while longer, stopping off and on to light incense.

I was giving myself five more minutes to power off. Hearing a soft, ruffled sound, didn't concern me, but new sounds were always tempting. I looked over my shoulder, not expecting anything unusual. I was stopped, frozen at the keyboard. Shaula Pearl was on my bed. This was a huge leap of enchantment. It brought me to my knees.

Anything that remotely changed her environment, even my voice, could tweak the moment. I took a chance. I said quietly, "Good girl. You look wonderful on the bed. Look. There's a pillow. It's yours." I should have known better, seeing how nervous she looked. She was back on her own bed within seconds, knocking her buffalo on the floor. Before I went to bed, I put the buffalo near her. He was becoming all too real to me.

I swore, the goddess mind would be hers. It was close. She wasn't rabbit queen, but she was buffalo queen. The enchantment plan was taking shape, becoming more defined with each passing month. The power behind words and actions were a large part of it. When I lost my dad, I heard a car horn, deep and croaky, at a gas station. I cried. When I was young, dad would pulled over at the side of the road, with me in the front seat, looking adoringly at cows in a pasture. He knew me. He would then get out of the car and blow a fog horn. All the cows would come running over. It was a lesson to me. If you care, show it.

The word turf was manifesting. The small bedroom was her domain, and she didn't hesitate to claim it. Rachael gave her the opportunity, walking Tala over to the house, her one year old German shepard who looked more like a big, black wolf. I was curious to see how Shaula Pearl would react in the presence of another dog. I felt nervous about it, aware of the X factor. I begged Rachael to hold the leash tight, as tight as the knot in my stomach. "If she lunges at Shaula Pearl," I told her, "I want you to throw yourself in-between them, and you will owe me orange cookies." It was a done deal.

Shaula Pearl was rummaging around in her closet, and it didn't sound thud friendly. When Tala entered the room, she backed into her closet, growling. It stunned me, again. I wasn't taking into account that it was her language and that she was a dog. She had more instinct than I gave her credit for. Tala remained calm and friendly, but Rachael led her out of the room, immediately. Enchantment had tagged her opinion. "I'm stressed. This is my space. I might bite."

Later that day, I took a walk around the neighborhood, trying to shed those few extra pounds that go away and come back. They miss me. I was missing a dog, padding along next to me, but it was okay. I loved her the way she was. I was proud of her, also. Voicing her opinion took courage. I walked on, running into Hazel, an old friend of mine, who lives on a hill near my neighborhood. It's sad how a hill became a reason for not seeing a friend. I felt guilty, but so did she. We hugged, with her old basset hound Mojo crammed between us, a sweet guy who pranced. We walked together for a few blocks, until Mojo stopped and growled at a dandelion. I laughed, it was so cute. Hazel told me that he always did that, and he growled at bushes and walls in their house. I was puzzled, never hearing about dogs growling at random objects. Hazel explained that Mojo was almost deaf, and sounds were confusing. He didn't trust the world like he used to.

We ending up in my driveway. I looked at my window, pointing to Shaula Pearl, the real one, who was staring at us over her shoulder. Hazel inquired if I had a couch under my window. I told her no, that Shaula Pearl was on my writing desk. Her eyebrows arched. There wasn't time for a full and enchanted explanation. I explained that my desk was large and strong enough to support her. I liked Hazel's comment. "May you always have someone who watches for you."

I replied back, "What a beautiful thought." Mojo had his opinion. He growled at my feet, sounding protective. He made a friend for life.

As we parted, Hazel made the comment, "You're nicer than me. Mojo isn't allowed on anything." I wanted to giggle, because he had thick, stocky legs. It would be hard to pounce higher than your knee.

"It's not a matter of being nice," I responded, hugging them both goodbye. "It's part of the enchantment plan. She does what she wants. It works for her."

"One lucky dog," Hazel said, over Mojo's growl. He was looking at a mushroom. After they left, I tip-toed upstairs with my camera, hoping she was still on the desk. Evidently, it was a great place for a princess flop.

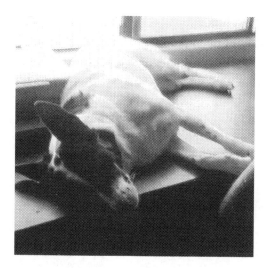

Hazel and I have much in common, but we see the world tilting our own way, which is the way it should be. One square foot of earth can be viewed so differently by someone else. I see a red leaf and a black stone. You see a snail and a berry. I see a dead beetle. You see a feather. We could argue about it an hour later. The important thing to remember, is respect. All realities, all personal truths, are all valid.

My vet has an interesting sleeping arrangement. He shares the bed with his wife and three beagles under the bedsheets. I know someone who puts her dog in the laundry room and goes to bed. I have a friend who puts her dog in pajamas. My mother spoon fed her dogs when they got old. Divine Light didn't write a book on how to take care of your dog, but supports books that speak of unconditional love. If your dog has that, it doesn't matter what pillow he claims. If you are ever at a loss for words, when someone challenges you on how you do things, quote A.A. Milne. "We can't all and some of us don't. That's all there is to it."

I attended a psychic fair recently, sitting with two readers at opposite ends of the room. The first reader asked me if I could accept the idea of a different reality, one that I couldn't see. It concerned my dog. I was intrigued, saying yes quickly. He then informed me that Shaula Pearl was not who she seemed to be on the outside. I readily agreed. What he said next, was a shocker. "She was a cat in her last life. She still has a lot of cat energy in her." What was even more surprising, was the next reader's comments. She looked me, cocking her head like a crow. I liked her for that. She simply stated, "You dog is a cat."

I'm an open-minded soul, but I have to say, I wasn't sure about this one. On the other hand, there are too many impossible thoughts already proven to be true. To name one, our Milky Way Galaxy is rotating its way through space at 330 miles per second. In one minute, we travel 12,000 miles. Don't ever let anyone tell you that you never go anywhere.

On that premise alone, I accepted their opinion, but also because Shaula Pearl seems to support it. She jumps effortlessly on anything flat and elevated. She sniffs me gently, up and down my arms and around my neck. She plays with paper bags, tissue paper and toilet rolls. She makes noises in her throat. She is an extremely finicky eater, passing up sizzling vegetarian meatballs but wolfing down tuna and grated cheese. She stares at me with that all-seeing, all-knowing cat look that makes you believe she could rule the world.

The fifth month gave me a scare from the feet up, although at this point, nothing should have unnerved me. The morning was going normal by new and enchanted standards. I got up and screamed. Instead of stepping on the carpet, I stepped on Shaula Pearl. She ran out of the room, crashing into her closet. I was beyond stunned. She slept by me. I never considered that happening. It was so normal. It was pack mentality, blossoming. It was so wonderful, believing that she wanted to be near me. It was human mentality, thriving. It was another enchanted moment that I messed up.

I celebrated without flashing disco balls, my first choice. I made chocolate chip muffins. Never hesitate to celebrate anything.

Celebrate an 'alive' day. Rejoice in moments. They are doorways to enchantment. Celebrate Shaula Pearl Day, August first, her assigned birthday. Eat toast. Bake cookies. Do what feels right. At night, Dream deep. Run breathless. Drink moonlight. Love effortlessly and without reason.

I don't know what came over me, but I consciously invited my friend Maura and her husband Bob over for dinner. I wondered if I could act normal, if I would sit on the rug with a paper plate, offering to share food. They came promptly at seven, walking in, hugging me, with no mention of the house. Maybe they were far sighted. Maura asked me if I made brownies. I had to laugh. It seems, it's all about chocolate.

After dinner, Maura and I caught up. Bob ate brownies. I finally gave in, talking about Shaula Pearl. She eats the house, because she needs to release all of her bunched up energy. She pulls off my bed sheets while I'm gone, but it reminds me to change them. She prances, discreetly at times, but it's only because, deep down, she is modest in her enchantment. Maura was intrigued with the word enchantment, asking me to explain it. I was about to say things like soul magic and healing energy, when the living room erupted, with of course, Shaula Pearl, at the epicenter. She was gurgling and howling at the same time. It was the strangest sound I had ever heard, outside of a werewolf movie.

We all froze, except for Shaula Pearl, who was doing this little dance with her paws and pretty much ignoring us. I began to wonder if she even knew we were there. Sleep walking crossed my mind. I spoke gently but firmly. "Shaula Pearl. It's okay. Go back upstairs." She froze this time, except for her tail, twitching like a cat. I tried the food decoy. "I'll get you a biscuit. Sit on my desk. Purr if you want." Now, she was completely still, sitting at the foot of the stairs, tilting slightly.

A moment later, she dropped something out of her mouth. Maura screamed. Bob grabbed a brownie for moral support. It looked like a dead rat from where we were sitting. Shaula Pearl ran behind the half gutted chair, sat for a second and then ran upstairs, banging into her closet. Maura poked me in the arm, saying to me, "Your dog. You look." It seemed fair. I walked over to the dead thing, half looking at it with one eye shut. I could see a black and a pink heart and a small heel.

"No way," I said, waving Maura over. "You have to see this." Maura came over reluctantly, making Bob go with her. "It's my valentine sock!" I yelled, a little too loud. Maura started to laugh, thank goodness. It saved the evening. I have no idea how Shaula Pearl found it. I keep my holiday socks in a heavy drawer under my emergency stash of dark chocolate.

After Maura and Bob left, I counted my holiday socks. They were all in my drawer, except for the one she had claimed, now in the washing machine. I live a life of constant amazement. Not only was Shaula Pearl playing, but it was on public display, nothing secretive about it. Joy was the magic word that night, in spite of one strange gurgle and a human scream. Joy to the world. Joy to Shaula Pearl. Joy to forgiving yourself for mistakes. Divine Light does. Regardless of the ones I've made, nothing seems to be stopping her from the realms of enchantment.

I study articles about dog research, not only for the sake of argument but to gain insight into the dog brain from the professionals and then delete what doesn't feel right. It's easy to experience cerebral overload when there are thousands of articles, all on the same subject. Coffee is good for you. It's bad for you. Two years later, it's good for you. I will never snub my nose at anyone's passion, for it is deeply rooted in their spirit. If you're obsessed with the mating rituals of cockroaches, and you write about it, so be it. If you're obsessed with enchanting paws and tails, so be it. Follow noble advice, listen to your gut and hear what your heart is saying. Sometimes, you grow into it.

I didn't have a clue when it came to love birds. I just wanted one. So I didn't check in with my gut. I went to a pet store, trusting the man behind the counter. He reassured me that I only needed to buy one and that my love bird would be blissfully content living with me. I believed him. He had the coat on and the name tag, and I liked his smile.

I brought my love bird home, attempting to make friends. I sat on the floor, placing the love bird and a plastic bird toy on my thigh. My love bird attacked the bobbing penguin, inflicting wounds before tossing it forcefully across the room. After that, he chased Mesa into the kitchen. He then chased me up the stairs, hopping at a frantic pace, hissing and possessed. I barely made it to the small bedroom, slamming the door shut. My love bird was thumping against the door with his body, trying to get me.

I brought my love bird back the next day. There was a new person behind the counter without a name tag. She explained to me that love birds like to be with other love birds. I needed to buy two. I felt bad, giving him back, but I only wanted one bird. There might have been a love bird in the store, who enjoyed human company, but there was too little time and too many love birds to figure it out.

I'm protective by nature, so the following day, I did research on love birds, defending the little goddess. They have their cuddly moments, but they are intense, fearless and prone to biting. Still, this world can be very unforgiving. You do a million things right and you get zero coverage. You do one thing wrong and it goes viral. That didn't happen, but I did receive a verbal bashing from someone at work for bringing my love bird back. I understand how it looked, but my gut was positive, someone else was fated to pursue flying penguins.

Animals should never be lumped together in a generic pile and given a label. I stuck to that. Love bird – not necessarily infected with genetic rabies. Individuality rules. Mesa hated to go to dog salons. Her first time was traumatizing for both of us. She was shaking while

I dropped her off, but I was positive that she would relax. I went to the bookstore, but my tea tasted anxious. I picked her up early. She was so distraught, she wouldn't give me eye contact. I groomed her at home. Wicca chased the wind and the rain, jumping as high as the back fence, so she remained inside during rainstorms. Shaula Pearl needs a quiet environment. I tether my joy close, so it doesn't scare her.

Shaula Pearl was feeling the word joy in small, juicy gushes. Love was the reason. Love magic. You can't enchant without it, and it needs to be real, not mechanical, devoid of feelings. There is an exception. I was in a blue funk one day, with no obvious reason why. I tried walking it off, ending up in a local thrift store. I thought of my mother who loved to hunt for vintage Miriam Haskell jewelry. I poked around for a bit, not seeing any. I was on the last aisle of the shop when I asked her to please send me a message, one that would lift my spirits. She was good at sending electrical messages, so I felt it was an easy request. She came through very cleverly. There was an old battery operated Barnie, off to my left. Barnie is a purple dinosaur, a popular TV character for many years. I smiled at him. He said, "You look beautiful." Thanks, mama. Never pass up a moment to enchant.

Just like the moon. She is there for everyone, enchanting without bias. The sun, with his scorching heart, warms everyone without judgment. Divine Light is for the enchantment of all souls. Equal light. Equal love. Equal rights. Animals are often excluded from this. As a result, animal shelters are full of lost and unwanted souls. Shelters take in around six to eight million dogs and cats every year in the United States. Close to three million animals are euthanized — the most common methods are by lethal injection or the gas chamber. Sometimes, the animals are forcibly held down in frightening positions. At the moment, Shaula Pearl is resting in her closet with a buffalo.

Think beautiful thoughts. They bounce. They create energy that hums and vibrates and are as powerful as the talons of an eagle. When directed, they have a mission and can help animals that are hurting. Positive energy carves a path to where it's needed, glowing with Divine Light, like the awe-inspiring tail of a shooting star.

"Supposing a tree fell down, Pooh, when we were underneath it."

"Supposing it didn't," said Pooh.

After careful thought, Piglet was comforted by this.

Five months in. Shaula Pearl looked charmed but tired. Closet living, panic attacks and munching on non-edible items, had taken its toll. But she had arrived at a place mentally, where she now believed in the possibility that she was safe. I sat with her often, inside of her thud inspired closet, enjoying the fact that it felt normal, plus the fact that she didn't seem to mind. I came bearing gifts, just in case. New fluffy socks were always appreciated.

The month was definitely a turning point. She had been hurt to the core but was embracing enchantment. She was beginning to realize that she was the keeper of her own soul, that the Garden of Eden, full of all things lovely and beautiful, existed inside of her. Discovering that sacred place, away from the physical landscape of the world, can be challenging. But she was doing it. I didn't know to what extent yet, but she was at the front gates, one paw in.

It became evident one night. I had closed the doggie door which I rarely do. It was cold and dark outside. I didn't want her out in the yard, siting in the ditch, while I took a shower. I was back at my desk in ten minutes. She snuck up behind me, silent as ever. My ghost girl. I knew she was there, only because she exhaled heavily. Grabbing my camera was more an intuitive move. The stirrings of magic were strong. Shaula Pearl was behind me with an expression that gives me, even today, the courage to do anything, to believe in myself, and in the dignity and splendor of all souls. It's her enchanted look, both paws in.

There was a reason for it. A huge lump of cotton was next to a paw. It had to be something colossal, a Godzilla sized catastrophe of pure joy. It was. Her bedroom was disemboweled. Her bedspread was on the floor. Her mattress was ripped open near the headboard, down to the coils. Her buffalo was under the pillow. Her throw rug was in her closet. A sock was hanging off the old computer desk in the corner of the room. Someone had a party in there while I was washing my hair.

I went to bed, too tired to converse with the dots. The clean-up job was minor, but when you're ready to collapse in bed, fluffing your pillow is taxing. Money was tight, but the look on Shaula Pearls face, was worth every one of the exposed coils.

CHAPTER TEN

JEWELS OF LIGHT

*"There are things that are known,
and things that are unknown, and
in between, there are doors."*
William Blake

One night, when Jasmyne was little, she curled up at the end of my couch, under a unicorn blanket, peering out of a small window in the living room. I joined her, wondering what she was looking at. She was caught in the grip of the full moon, in all her of beguiling enchantment. We talked about it in whispers, why it glowed and how big it was. We fell asleep together for over an hour. We looked out the window again, and the sky was moonless. It was magic to Jasmyne. She was right. It was divine magic. The blue marble of our earth, churning around and around, creating the illusion that the moon travels across the night sky as the earth sleeps.

I told her that I loved the unknown, the mysterious, that it always led me to the light of things. She smiled, asking me to make cinnamon toast. We glowed in the light of the grill, melting butter and cinnamon sugar, marveling at the scent as we opened the oven door. We had no fears that night.

Dark chocolate makes any negative situation beautiful, so why not have it every day, just in case? It is one of the most priceless blessings, to have options and be able to act on them. Shaula Pearl had been living with me now for five months, with soft, new friends and safe places to explore. She could choose her preferences. Perhaps only to emphasize it, I had some fun with her. I placed two dog biscuits on

129

a paper plate and waited. One of them was smeared in peanut butter and one with Velveeta cheese. She stared at them like they were cast in gold. Drool was dripping. She lustfully went for the cheese biscuit, pounding into her bedroom. There was no time for a prance with heaven in your mouth.

Shaula Pearl, with all of her enchanting choices, was folding out of her chrysalis, with thick layers of dust and dirt, scattering. Her transformation, from stone dog to prance dog, was far from what I had expected. I believed strongly that she would heal, but I was amazed at how fast it was happening. I had forgotten how love can build worlds.

In the sixth month, change, anywhere in the house, was still close to intolerable. My purse was scary. If I put it somewhere unusual, anywhere but the bathroom counter, she looked at it suspiciously, backing up. Bags from the market needed to be emptied quickly and put away. Clothes items were hung up after I took them off. I couldn't leave things out, like vacuums or brooms or a stack of towels. Even so, she tolerated a few things that were new. My goose-necked lamp went unnoticed. The new bean bag in the living room was ignored.

It's hard to explain what bothers her and what doesn't – and why. But abuse is private. To survive it, you shift things around in your head until you feel deceivingly comfortable, or numb. Think of it this way. You're trapped in a small room, for years, with at least twenty other people who are as frightened as you are. You can't move much, maybe a leg. Someone comes in every day and throws rocks at you or scares you in the middle of the night with a blast of water. Mentally, you shut down. One day, without warning, someone pulls you out, puts you in a van and takes you to a recovery program. Then, a human takes you home and tells you that she wants to enchant you. Right. Why would you believe the human? Why would you believe the coat draped over the banister. Everything is out to get you.

I had dinner with a colleague that I hadn't spoken with for at least a year. She had been overseas studying early childhood programs. At first, we talked about catching up stuff — families, anti-depressants and body imperfections. Details of her trip followed. I listened raptly for over an hour. When she finished, she cordially asked me what I was up to, beyond the 'stuff.' I looked at her with a twinkle in my eye. "I'm enchanting someone," I said. She put her coffee mug down hard, getting visibly excited.

"Who is he? Why didn't you tell me about him?" she practically yelled, shuffling papers into her briefcase.

"Well. I date once in a while, but that's not it. It's not a he." I realized what I had said, looking at her expression. "Zero tolerance for judging," I said. "It doesn't matter who we love, but that we love."

"I get that! Who is it?" she blurted out, smashing her car keys on the table. "I'm not leaving until you tell me."

"Calm down. It's a dog," I answered, beaming now.

"Oh," was all she said, still looking surprised. I launched into a fifteen minute explanation, with pictures, demonstrated gurgles, glow fur highlights and spiritual messages. I was drooling. When I finished, she wanted to meet Shaula Pearl and went on to describe some methods of enchantment that she felt would help, drawing on her own wealth of child development. I listened with enthusiasm, deleting the ones that I didn't like. I appreciated my friend. If you can excite interest, you add flame to the fire. You add passion to the cause.

I drove home with the moon chasing me - a jewel, pinned against the breast of the sky. The sun was leaving his day throne, melting into a palette of colors. I couldn't see the stars yet, but I knew they were there, the silent guardians of the day, lifting their veils at night. Light is everywhere. Inside of us. Outside of us. Above us and below us. It hit me then, on that drive home, during the sixth month of my new and enchanted life, that I lacked nothing, that I had everything. I saw a sunflower at the side of the rode, its face, with an aura of yellow petals, bent and heavy with seeds, stood proud. It was Shaula Pearl, with her so called flaws that made perfect.

I thought of a sweet friend, when I was attending college, who was born without any arms or legs. She liked to sit on the ledge of her window, in her dorm room, and watch students walk by. One day, she told me about all the well-meaning suggestions about her life, what to do with it and how to do it. But she knew, that you live in your own enchantment. She told me that she had listened, gathered what was helpful and set her own sails, off on her own journey. What I remember most about her, was not only her strength but her sense of humor. I walked into her room one morning, offering to make her bed so her feet wouldn't get cold. Foot in mouth. I was horrified at what I said. She thought it was funny and couldn't stop laughing.

The day ended by moonlight flooding the room. Instead of writing, I did goddess things like paint my toenails and dabble in my essential oils. I read for a while, occasionally glancing up, looking for Shaula Pearl who was out and about exploring something. We were so much alike. She liked adventure, I could tell. So did I. She had fears. I had my own, besides urban legends of lost feet. She had wants, a never ending supply of socks. I wanted new jeans with intentional holes, new nail polish that wasn't clumpy and a new can of soda.

By the time I got to the kitchen, I realized that Shaula Pearl was outside. I could see her silhouette on the wood planks, glowing as usual. It occurred to me that she rarely went into yard, unless I walked her out, or she panicked, barreling through the doggie door. I watched her from the kitchen, afraid that if I moved closer, she would come back in. She wasn't alone, either. There were trails of light, racing back and forth, the length of the yard. Angels came to mind, but the lights had the shape of animals with tails. Mesa and Wicca were outside, running around the yard. I took a picture of the dirt and the sky, hoping to catch them on camera. Instead, I found a rabbit orb in a palm tree. Life makes me grin. Uno was in the yard, watching the festivities.

The rational world plays with our imagination. The fleeting glint of a bejeweled dragonfly, mistaken for a fairy. The face of an old man inside a crystal. The shape of an angel in tree bark. The world itself, is a massive orb hurtling through space, while we sit and read books and bake cookies. How wild is that?

Seeing Uno, glowing as an orb rabbit, was certainly wild but not impossible. The spiritual realms slip into our physical world all the time. Glow Uno will always remind me of Mesa, but on this enchanted evening, I thought of Wicca and the unexpected ways that spirit can manifest.

Wicca and I would take early morning walks before I would leave for work. You get to know the people and dogs in your neighborhood. If there are newcomers on the cement trails, you pick them out pretty quickly. One particular morning, it was colder than usual. I had a bowl of hot cereal with chocolate chips added to make me brave. Cold and I are not friends. Now, mentally I was ready. After only a short block, a lady jogged by us at a fairly good speed. That wasn't so unusual, but what she did was odd. She looked at me over her shoulder and yelled, "Go back home! A loose Rottweiler is running your way, and he hasn't been neutered!" I didn't know what to think.

First, I had never seen her before. Second, she had knowledge about the dog that most people wouldn't have noticed, especially on a run. And third, why would she bother to tell me anyways? She didn't know me or Wicca and that she was a girl, weak from cancer.

She stopped jogging, looking at me again, firmly advising me to get back to my house. As she took off, she yelled the word, "Now!" At that point, I understood. She was an angel, forewarning me of very unpleasant events, soon to manifest. I urged Wicca to walk at a brisk pace, noticing the shape of a dog, a few blocks away, hurtling towards us like a runaway train. I will be forever be grateful for the jogging angel that morning who had our backs.

People kept asking me about bonding. Have you bonded yet? Has she bonded with you? It's hard to recap six months, so I would say, rather mysteriously, "Yes. We have a close attachment to each other in strange and extraordinary ways." I got questions after that, but it was all good. Curiosity is a normal obsession. I have it. I wonder why some people get dogs. At the same time, I understand. Your level of bonding with an animals involves your own personal experiences, your own upbringing.

Still, I am very suspicious of the word. "Yes, I bond with my dog. I feed him and let him out. I buy him toys. I don't really play with him. I don't have time. Yes, I bond with my dog, but I had a baby. I can't take care of them both. Yes, I have three dogs. I have their photos all over my work desk. I'm moving to a smaller house, easier to clean. I won't have room for all of them. I'm leaving one with my good friend. Really?

I have to admit, I am guilty of this one in my early twenties. "Yes, I love my dog. I wasn't ready for my own dog. I gave him away." I was living away from home, out-of-state, barely out of college and broke. I lived in a small house with a girlfriend who was just like me. That was scary. We both loved brownies, boyfriends and flowers in our hair. I was lonely though, because I wanted a dog. It was always about dogs. One day, I was walking home from work and there were large, fluffy puppies, prancing all over someone's yard. I grabbed one with permission. I didn't have a leash or a dog bowl or a dog bed. At that point in my life, I did things with my heart always in the lead.

I named her T.J. She grew fast, a wholly bear at six months. I wasn't prepared for her. I was too unbridled in the joy department. We were two wild souls having a heck of a good time. I was busy with my life. T.J. spent the day running exuberantly everywhere, jumping over ducks and barreling down country paths. She always came back, and we would snuggle and play all night long. I took her home for a month, and she ate my mother's lemon meringue pie and her chicken dinner and ran all over the house in wild, shameless joy.

My mother wrote often, filling up journals, highlighting family events, plus her own thoughts - most likely where I inherited the habit. I found a notebook about T.J. years after the fact. In her words, she said, "My daughter brought home a stuffed animal looking dog, towering over my shepherds. She was a lovable, nutty, bumbling, destructive and undisciplined. She tore up one of my chairs. She drank water with such abandonment, it splashed in every direction for three or four feet."

Before I left, I listened to my parents. I gave her away to a great family. I still feel insanely guilty about it. I also know that we can't help who we are, at certain times in our lives, but when we figure it out, we can make better choices and promise to help others. Shaula Pearl and I were ready for each other, but I was the one who had to be grounded enough. Joy, and a strong sense of self, plus the ability to see outside of yourself, makes for a good partnership.

During the sixth month, evenings were predictable to a point, with me at the writing desk and Shaula Pearl in her room with her sock and buffalo. One evening, I needed a break from thinking, so I just sat, staring out my window, watching the sky darken. The sun was descending, splashing colors around like a wild painter. The delicate veil of twilight and the denser shawl of night, were battling it out, fighting for their time. I was enjoying the view when a lady stopped for a moment, at the foot of my driveway, talking to her dog who was on a leash, not enchanted. Shortly after, she began to walk slowly, yanking on the leash, trying to get her dog to cooperate and walk by her legs. I admit, it's a good goal, but not the hurtful and annoying part. Her dog was coughing constantly. It looked more like a power struggle than a training session.

The dog didn't seem to have a clue what the lady wanted or was simply ignoring her. He went into dog mode. He sniffed at the grass. The lady yelled, "Stop it. You're being stupid. Bad dog!" Her voice carried itself through a three inch opening in my window. That did it. It was none of my business, but I got up, walked downstairs rather quickly and went outside, knowing that my foot was already crammed in my mouth. I said hello to her. She nodded her head, without smiling.

I took that as a conversation. I said to her, "I used to have one of those leashes. I switched over to a harness. It pulls on the chest. It's more comfortable for the dog, and it makes you less frighteningly clueless." That's not what I said, but I was thinking it. I told her that I was only speaking from experience, knowing that choking was a bad feeling. The ice cube memory. I was hoping to extend the conversation, but she thanked me and left. Her dog seemed happier, though. He looked at me and grinned. He knew what I knew – that he was there to teach her something. As dogs do, he took it in stride.

Shaula Pearl, with all of her joy potential, would not be aspiring to enchantment, if she didn't feel loved. The lady with the leash, very well might have loved her dog, but the quality of our time with our animals, even moments, are so critical to their well-being. Shaula Pearl didn't see Jasmyne very often, maybe on the weekends, but whenever she did, Jasmyne was always quiet and respectful in her presence. One night, we had a slumber party. Jasmyne slept at the side of my bed, on a mattress. During the night, Shaula Pearl came into the room, sniffing her feet. I happened to wake up and witness it. The following morning, she pranced into the bedroom, stopping in front of Jasmyne, who had just opened her eyes. I whispered, "Don't move. It's an enchanted moment." Jasmyne was smart and didn't listen to me. She petted her. I was stunned, grabbing my camera off the nightstand. Love makes you feel strong and brave.

When Jasmyne was five, she experienced the power of love in a very unexpected way. We were on a road trip, traveling with Wendi from California to Indiana. Wendi was driving, and Jasmyne and I were in the backseat, holding onto each other. There was a terrifying wind storm, pushing the car around like it weighed a feather. The highway was very narrow, fueling my fears. The wind would shove us into oncoming traffic, crushing us. I was saying prayers in my head repeatedly, asking for angelic assistance. Jasmyne began tapping me on the shoulder saying, "Look, grandma. Look." I dismissed her, too concerned about the wind and keeping a vigilant eye on the traffic.

The following morning, we checked out of our motel, early. Jasmyne asked me, discreetly, if I would like to know what she was trying to tell me. I told her, of course I did, apologizing at the same time, knowing that it was late, but better than nothing. I had been stuck in the moment, the adult moment of worry. What Jasmyne told me, made me feel even worse. She had witnessed an enchanted moment, and the opportunity was gone for her to share it with me. A woman's face had been outside the car, looking at her through a window, the one next to me. She described the woman as having a kind face, surrounded by golden hair, and the women was smiling at her. An angle was there protecting us, making Jasmyne feel safe.

The sixth month molded me into a better enchantress, learning more about her, basically what she liked and didn't like. Cardboard boxes were high on her priority list. If the box was too large, it would go unharmed. She favored brown paper bags over gift bags. She liked the sofa chair to be a few feet away from the back wall, so she could walk around it. What she didn't like, were flat parcel envelopes and cereal boxes with the plastic lining intact. She turned her nose up at egg cartons, brownie boxes and candy boxes. The scent alone should have been enticing, but like anyone else, she has her preferences.

I was also learning what I could do, without Shaula Pearl revising it in some way. I repositioned my three foot tall oriental vase, previously on the floor by the fireplace, to the wall by the entrance hall. I placed fake long-stemmed flowers in it, sticking out at odd angles which felt familiar. It now stood by a small antique table with candles on it. I stood back, eyeing it with approval. I had created a small, charming space within my joyously ravaged house.

The morning had a different opinion. The vase was toppled over with an original design of tiger lilies, by Shaula Pearl, decorating the kitchen floor, slathered in dry dog saliva and frayed at the edges. I didn't give up. I replaced the flowers and moved the vase by the gutted chair, putting a stuffed bear in front of it. She left the vase alone, moving the bear from one place to another, usually at night.

It was a constant balancing act of needs and wants. I wanted her to go on a walk. I wanted to walk with her. I wanted. I leashed her up, promising her an extraordinary outdoor experience. I opened the front door, pushing her out gently. We walked to the driveway on slow mode. A gardener rounded the corner of my townhouse and said hi. Shaula Pearl gurgled. He smiled, patting his thigh, asking her to come over. At the same time, a gardener, who was across the street, turned on his leaf blower. Shaula Pearl screeched, sounding like a barn owl. My want was not her need. I belly walked her in. I rubbed her sock and her buffalo with lavender oil. I played her favorite CD. I turned off lights and lit candles. She forgave me, being the sweet soul that she is.

It's hard enough, removing myself from the physical world, and all of its enthralling accessories, balancing out my own wants and needs. Joy to whatever you desire, if it doesn't hurt anyone, or yourself. I stared at a large fake plant, in the aisle of a home décor store, admiring its deep purple leaves. I wanted it. I checked the price tag a few times, in the same five minutes, stubborn as usual. The price didn't change. It didn't matter. I needed it to be happy. If I had this plant, life would be great, and all of my issues would go away. I also wanted the heat to go on next month. I didn't buy it. The same week, I wanted to change my kitchen. I bought a gallon of purple paint, going a little hog wild, painting the walls and the ceiling. It was the better choice. We ate the next month. I held back on movies and sushi. I bought one package of California rolls at the market, but they don't count.

Shaula Pearl was actively seeking joy. She would sniff all over the house, searching for socks. I hid them well, but it was more of a game. She was also getting braver, pouncing on gift bags. Poking me was happening, almost daily, while I was writing. She was a white tiger on silent paws, inching closer and closer to her prey – me. Without warning, she would dash forward, poking me on the side, with her nose sticking through the metal arms of my swivel chair. It birthed another promise. If I was kissing the rose red lips of my vampire with his silken hair, dark as crow feathers, scented with wild rose petals, I would stop writing and pet her. She was finally at ease with that. But I can't say it was easy. Writers have possessed fingers on a keyboard.

No matter what else she did, asking for a touch was monumental. It was an act of grace, a jewel of light, glowing in the garden of her mind. More were growing, I could tell. Light creates light, sparking and igniting hope. Brushwood was burning in her soul, soon to be a forest fire. Joy exploding. It was coming.

For now, rubbing her neck and her chest was amazing, in itself, and dog friendly. Patting the top of the head can be easily misread. A shy dog can take it as an aggressive move. It doesn't feel good, either. Pat the top of your head. It feels like a lead ball smashing your brain. Also, rubbing her belly was a hope, but for now, it was too vulnerable a position. Eventually, I felt she would go for it. It was a feel good event. In dogs, brain neurons respond to hair follicles. A belly rub stimulates joy sensors. Humans are the same way. Stroking a babies cheek or rubbing their belly, enhances healthy emotional development.

With that in mind, I touched her whenever I could. The stalking of the white tiger was increasing. I was beginning to catch her at it, but it was more fun when she surprised me. It was a great big point for dog's demonstrating affection without any other agenda. Shaula Pearl didn't ask for a biscuit. She didn't want me to play, because she didn't play with anyone but herself. She wasn't asking to go on a walk. She wanted my touch.

Hippos. I thought of them one night, watching Shaula Pearl prance into the living room, her massive neck, jiggling at a good pace, making her head bob up and down. Size doesn't matter when it comes to a joy dance. I observed that at a zoo, watching a hippo in an underwater enclosure. He was eight thousand pounds, a big hefty male, but he was dancing underwater as delicate as a ballet performer. I stared at him in total admiration, feeling bad that I had assumed, it was beyond his ability to move without clumping along. How easily we describe an animal or a person with one word, one adjective, ignoring all of their other wonderful attributes. We make judgments on one part of a whole. How ludicrous. Dumb dog. Clumsy Hippo. Contented cow. Shaula Pearl sat by her food bowl, watching me pour an uncalculated amount of chocolate chips into a bowl of oatmeal cookie dough. Closet dog. Anti-social dog.

Later that evening, it poured. Large, plump raindrops pelted the house, justifying my need to bake. Time to celebrate anyways. It was rain. Rain is the child of grace, growing the colors of the earth. I sat on my bed, leaning against the back wall, trying to salvage crumbs, and listening to the wild soul of the storm, hissing and snarling. The wind was howling like a banshee. The heat went on, purring like a Cheshire cat, with its invisible magic, warming my cold nose.

I felt compelled to look. My street was a churning cauldron of storm energy, toppling over trashcans and whipping grass and twigs into a frenzy. It looked joyous to me, including my window. It was beautiful. Brown and green leaves, dark pink flower petals and feathery white seeds, were smashed against glass. It was a painting that could rival the wild landscapes of Rousseau.

With storm driven thoughts, I was close to falling asleep, sure that my dreams would be spellbound, when I heard a thud. Nothing usual about that. It wasn't enough to worry me. Two thuds later, I opened my eyes. On the count of three thuds, I sat up. It was time to investigate. Shaula Pearl wasn't upstairs, so I walked down carefully, since random objects appear on them overnight, from silverware to sponges. On this darksome night, there was only a buffalo.

A quick glance around the room, proved nothing. I checked the obvious, the garage, yard and closet, followed by the unobvious, the fireplace and the oven. I was beginning to feel anxious when the kitchen ceiling began to vibrate. She was evidently in the middle bedroom. Like I said, she's magic. I didn't see her when I was upstairs. But there she was, sitting on the bed, next to my brown stuffed Labrador, now missing an eyeball. I could deal with that. She had gone into another room that had previously frightened her. She was playing, damage assessment normal. "You want both bedrooms?" I asked her, trying not to feel sentimental over the eyes. The dog looked like Mesa, or had. The bottom line was, she could have most everything she wanted except my Halloween socks. Those were sacred.

The following morning, I spent some time in the backyard picking up trash, the wind had so generously blown over the fence. The dirt was soft and wet from the rain. My toes were enjoying it, their own personal spa. I sat for a while, at the foot of my thirty year old friend, a queen palm, with her smooth gray trunk and large canopy of feathery plumes. I listened to her. She was singing with the wind, swishing and rustling her jade green leaves, glazed with water droplets. I wondered if she ever wanted to rip up her roots and run. She told me no, that she was a part of the earth, of the space she lived in. She felt strong, rooted in the rich browns of the earth and in the dark reds and grays of deep soil, with small crumbled rocks glistening with quartz. She was at peace with herself.

My hopes for Shaula Pearl were identical. For the moment, at least, she was in a far better place than she had been. I looked at her, in awe of most everything she did, even tracking a fly. It was another great moment of normalcy. Then, she sniffed at a dandelion and a small patch of grass and Wicca's old toy. She paused, looking up, sniffing seeds, cottony and yellow. She was enjoying herself. A small gust of wind blew through the yard, sending her inside. She came back out, seconds later, walking over to me, poking me on the arm. No chair between us. It was one small, enchanted moment, as simple as it gets, but one that I will never forget.

"Pooh," he whispered.

"Yes, Piglet?"

"Nothing," said Piglet, taking Pooh's paw.

"I just wanted to be sure of you."

CHAPTER ELEVEN

FEARS BECOMING FLOWERS

*"Live in the sunshine. Swim the
seas. Drink the wild air."*
Ralph Waldo Emerson

I sat on soft springy sand, the chest of the sea, listening to her seductive voice, wet and raspy, swirling and frothy, a passionate sermon of many dialects, speaking to the violet face of the sky and the crowd of palm trees, standing reverently in the open corridors of the earth's temple. I said a prayer to the whales. The sea was grateful. She left me trinkets that she treasured, far more than ships, laden with trunks of jewels – a seashell with a galaxy spiraling on its back, a purple-red rock, polished by the rags of the tides, and one small sand dollar. All the wealth of the world was at my feet.

I looked at the sea and had no words, for an emerald green sea dragon rose with rainbow scales and golden talons. His eyes were the light of stars, and his wings were amethyst. He rose higher, arching his back and then dipping deep into the violet stained sea, his baptismal font. He rose again, but this time, he kept ascending, higher and higher, looking back at me once, asking me what I believed in. I said, "love." He said, "That is my Kingdom."

Love is a warrior when you need a shield and a sword. Fighting the enemy, Shaula Pearl's memories, and defending her right to be enchanted, was a daily battle. The seventh month brought a great victory, slightly unusual in the way it played out, but it was a win anyways. It was an act of courage, focus and willful intent, plus some red sauce.

My friends were begging for a scary movie. We voted for a charming and compelling creature of the night, thin crust pizza with pineapple and a chocolate dessert bar. I fear a life without chocolate, so I have to make sure I indulge at a fairly consistent rate. There were no complaints from my friends. Chocolate was a bonding experience, one that I was not suspicious of.

The evening was sweetly fear-provoking. We were in the movie, walking with our creature, deep in the bowels of his gilded castle, lined with Persian rugs and drugged by the minty, honey laden scent of eucalyptus oil. He was convincing us that our crumbling mortals lives could be filled with night flights and nocturnal promises. He could charm a cobra. We believed him, gulping down chocolate pastries in my concrete townhouse, damaged beyond my immediate funding. With endorphins on the rise, no one seem to care.

Shrouded in our own moon spun mist, we were oblivious to the creature on the stairs, tilting. I noticed her first, aware of her energy. I took her picture without alerting my friends. No sense in disturbing their enchantment.

What happened next, truly shocked me. She pranced down, and with the grace of a princess, put the edge of Belinda's paper plate, delicately in her mouth, with her slice of pizza on it, and pranced upstairs. I was speechless. My friends were staring at me, waiting for an explanation. I didn't have one. Six months ago, breathing was an effort. This evening, she claimed her inner dog goddess. She heard her own mantra, "You are worthy of pizza." As she disappeared into her closet, it never occurred to me that I should scold her. This was a major event when it came to enchantment. She smelled food. She trusted me enough to trust everyone else. No one had ever told her that it was rude to eat pizza without asking.

Anger is pointless. I was sitting in a café, drinking a chocolate banana smoothie, mentally willing the calories away from my hips. There was a small child wobbling by me, carrying a porcelain plate with a large cookie on it. His mother was a few feet in front of him, headed to a table. The child tripped on nothing, something toddlers and I have in common. The plate hit the floor, breaking into small pieces, followed by the cookie. His mother turned around, saying loudly, "Why did you do that? There's glass everywhere. I have to buy another cookie."

The cookie. It was high on her priority list. The little boy cringed and began to cry. I came very close to intervening, but knew the trouble I would get in. Parenting is personal and is not considered abusive if you don't leave any marks. But a mark had been left. His ego was crushed. He didn't do anything wrong. You don't give a breakable plate to a young child and the responsibility of getting it somewhere safely. He was set up, as unintentional as it was. The mother got it. She hugged him, asking him if he would like to help with the mess. He smiled, putting a small piece of cookie in his mouth. No one scolded him.

I enchanted daily without trying to be neurotic about it. Even so, I would cringe if my goblet clanked down too hard on my desk, or I slammed my closet door shut with too much energy. It was easy to do now, since the doorknob had somehow mysteriously fallen off and disappeared. It wasn't in her closet. I concentrated on being myself, but at the same time, aware that my actions had to be tempered with a constant mindfulness of where she was and what she was doing.

One night, I came home very late and very exhausted. I put on my happy voice, greeting her, although I had a sneaky feeling, she could see right through it. I shut the door way too loud and stomped upstairs, grumbling like a hungry bear. I flung my purse on the bed, growling at the contents spilling out. I snapped at my nail file, asking it rudely, why I could never find it. I kicked off the bricks holding my feet down and unfastened the ten pound weight belt around my waist. I felt beaten. Work can do that, if you spent the day with a visiting human who believes that good is shredding your self-esteem and bad is not having enough cream in her coffee. I needed a hot shower to slush of any dark energy clinging to me. Instead, I switched into my comfy attire, fed Shaula Pearl and collapsed on the bed yelling, "I can't move! I'll get up in a few minutes!"

I fell asleep and woke up twenty minutes later. I still didn't get up. It felt liberating to do nothing. I gave myself ten more minutes to luxuriate in nothing. I finally got up, hearing a soda fizzing my name. I shuffled into the hallway, feeling less human and more sloth-like. I wasn't paying attention, either. I tripped on nothing, falling into the guard rail, plunging down and doing a half somersault on top of the buffalo. I screamed. Shaula Pearl was sitting at the top of the stairs, and she screamed, bashing into her closet. I needed lessons from the hippo – and yes, you might tag me as frighteningly clueless in the aware department. I am the professor who trips over a chair and bangs her head on the overhead projector.

That evening, I was mad at myself for a couple of reasons. I had given my work day 'power.' I should have come home, lit sage, danced with my one-eyed Labrador and taken a hot, steamy shower. I should have checked my directions from the bed to the hallway with both eyes opened. Be aware at all times, was now a new mantra. It's a good one, but hard to do.

I almost lost Wendi, by not paying attention, and she is priceless to me. I took her to the mall when she was two. We were having a great time, until I dropped her hand, zipping my purse shut. It was plenty of time for a toddler to vanish. I panicked, running into a store and commanding a lady, behind a counter, to grab a loud speaker and alert the entire mall, and surrounding countryside, that she was missing. Immediately after, I ran down the mall, screaming her name, looking everywhere at once like a human owl. We were all lucky. A security guard found her. She was crying, my heart was bleeding, and I swore, I would never zone out again, at least, with a family member.

Shaula Pearl was family. I crawled into her bedroom, begging forgiveness. Being a soul who was tolerant of my flaws, she forgave me as usual. I told her that my gravestone should read, "What was I thinking." The t-shirt I would insist on wearing, would say, "I meant well." I also wanted a sign posted saying, 'Don't cut the grass.' It would grow thick and abundant, a grassy legacy of wild soul energy in full joy. She looked at me and snuffed. I sat with her for a while, silencing my thoughts, soaking up her positive energy. Pooh snuck in with his gentle wisdom. "Always watch where you are going. Otherwise, you might step on a piece of the forest that was left out by mistake." I agreed, blaming my feet of course, giving them fair warning that I would hang them over the mattress if they ever scared her again.

The next night, I opened the front door in full intentional focus. I imagined my carpet smelling like a Hawaiian island. I saw a chocolate fountain built into the kitchen. I looked up, covering the hallway with exotic runners. Instead, my comforter was there, all bunched up, looking more like a tent. There was another party in the house. I can't fault her.

Upon closer inspection, the downstairs had taken on another home interior design. It was Art Deco with a touch of Hansel and Gretel. There was a trail of random objects in the living room, circling around the big chair and up the stairs, consisting of vintage oracle cards and some kitchen appliances such as my egg beater and a wooden spoon. The drawers were open in the kitchen, explaining the cooking paraphernalia. I went upstairs looking for her. She came prancing out of her room, giving me a look that said, "What? Everything's fine here."

That wasn't the end of it. She was bursting with enchanted energy, releasing it everywhere, particularly in my room. Maybe that was a compliment. My sheets and blankets were off the bed. They were draped over my desk and nightstand. I needed to wash them anyways. Her dog bed was upside down with a hole in the middle of it. Okay. I could patch it up. My pillow was on top of her crate without injuries. My house phone was pulled out of the socket, half chewed. I wanted to cancel service anyways, since I never used it. I worked my way through that one.

Discipline is challenging without any enchantment issues. Link the crime to the punishment. Play the matching game. If your four year old rides his bike in the street, take his bike away, not his basketball. If your dog makes dinner on his own, proudly presenting it to you as you get home from work, your favorite shoe gnawed to the bone, put it somewhere inaccessible and give him something he can chew on. With dogs, they won't get it unless you catch them in the act. Shaula Pearl was the classic example. She never partied seriously while I was watching. I couldn't reprimand her, after the fact, for having a really fun day. No fairness in that.

I had an unsettling thought, and it wasn't the first one. I would have to leave her, at some point, and that point was coming in a few weeks. I was spending Thanksgiving with Wendi, who was still living in Indiana. I was having mental seizures, one after the other, afraid that she would feel abandoned or try to escape. I came up with a plan. Beg angels for non-stop assistance. Hide everything I wanted to have when I returned. Tape drawers shut. Remove oven knobs, since she turned on the gas once, and close all doors, placing emergency tape across them.

A teacher at work, who was also a good friend, knew I was worried. She walked into my office with something under her jacket and kicked my door shut. Without asking permission, she opened a bottle of Kahlua, pouring some in my coffee. What kind of boss would allow that? I thanked her, giggling, but it came out more like a gurgle. "Don't mention it," she said, patting her heart. "I know what you're going through. You can fire me if you want."

"Not today," I stated, trying to maintain an air of authority.

I packed the next night, explaining to Shaula Pearl that I was going on a trip, that she would be safe and that Rachael would be feeding her. It was a hard night. The suitcase frightened her. She wouldn't come into my room until I placed it in the bathroom, where I ended up packing it. I dropped my flat iron. That startled her. She curled up in her closet, refusing to come out for the rest of the evening. I was feeling anxious. She felt it. I sprayed her buffalo with lavender oil and put it under her chin. She snuffed, pawing my arm. I sprayed myself.

I called Julia, who gave me a great suggestion. The first night I was in Indiana, she told me to picture the moon, passing over my house. After that, I should mentally say, "Shaula Pearl. Five more nights, and mommy will be home. According to Julia, I should do this every night, preferably in bed when the house was quiet. The following night would be four nights. I should continue this visualization until the last night I was there. She assured me that Shaula Pearl would hear me, see the image of the moon, in the night sky, and understand that I would be coming home after so many nights. Before hanging up, I asked her to please alert Shaula Pearl that I was leaving for Indiana early in the morning. Julia told me that she had been aware of my trip, a few months ago. She knew the shuttle was coming soon. She knew everything.

I left at three in the morning, tripping over a buffalo on the stairs. I thanked it for not breaking my leg. I didn't want to leave with any negative energy in the house. I focused on Wendi's genetic ability to bake perfect brownies, and my charming granddaughter Ayva, who will enchant this world. I had a wonderful visit. At night, I took Julia's advice. In the privacy of their guest room, Shaula Pearl and I would do a moon count down. Following that, I would tell her about my day, shifting into an Alpha state, connecting with her on a much deeper level. Alpha is a brain wave cycle, calming your mind and body, but at the same time, allowing you to remain in a state of alertness. Science and magic are the same thing. Brainwaves and altered states. We do it all the time. We alpha when we daydream or zone out joyfully, dancing, meditating or drumming. I alpha when I eat dark chocolate.

Alpha is an enchanting experience. I alpha in bed, listening to angelic music. I didn't bring any, so I engaged in a visualization that I enjoy – The Rose Gateway. I lie in bed, visualizing a large white rose, the size of a dinner plate, a foot above me. After that, the rose changes color, following the pattern of our chakras. I breathe in the colors, slowly and deeply. First, I inhale red. On the next inhale, the rose turns orange. I continue to fill myself with colors, becoming yellow and green, and then blue, indigo and violet. After violet, the rose becomes white again. On the next inhale, it fades into my body, filling me with Divine Light. After that, I continue to relax and breathe deeply, concentrating on what I'm seeking. Often, I ask for guidance on what I'm writing about. Other times, I ask for a message from my mother or deceased husband or even a message from one of my dogs. Once, I asked my guide to reveal his or her name. Of course, I wanted to know what it was, instantly. I entered an alpha state for five nights. Finally, I heard the name Gabriel, whispered in my good ear. Patience might have been the lesson.

The second night, all I wanted to do was send Shaula Pearl love, streams of it, flowing all over my house, with an over-abundance of exuberance, as usual. Hot pinks and magentas shot out into the night sky of Indiana, soaring off to California. I added a few neon purples, knowing that purple was a familiar color. I got more than I bargained for. There was a flash of light out of the corner of my eye. "Please don't let my retina detach in my daughter's bed," I said, recalling an eye issue in my human development text book.

Somebody was listening. There was Shaula Pearl, standing at the side of my bed. She vanished a moment later. I was stunned at her presence but also with the realization that animals could astral project, leave their physical body and travel in their astral body, as we can. I was reminded of the term disassociation, removing yourself mentally during repeated trauma. I had a feeling, Shaula Pearl had taken it a step further, removing herself physically from her abuse.

I had one more surprise waiting for me in the morning. I got an amazing update from Rachael. Shaula Pearl was out of her closet and downstairs, acting playful. I was more stunned with this information than with Shaula Pearl flying to Indiana. She was trusting Rachael. It made sense. Rachael is one of my puppies. The only issue that came up, was her eating and drinking on the fourth night. My heart was beginning to ache. I could feel her missing me.

After my trip, Shaula Pearl would come downstairs when Rachael was over. She favored dinner time, and would stand by her, stiff and wide eyed, watching her eat.

I attended a workshop for psychic development, a year ago. The person in charge, requested that we share anything interesting or unusual during the course of the workshop. The man sitting next to me, introduced himself as an energy healer and psychic by profession. He stated that a dog was standing in front of him, but the dog was still very much alive. He described her as being white with large black spots, plus a long bushy tail and large ears. He talked about her body shape and her legs and how her belly hung down a little. It was Shaula Pearl. What a great confirmation that she had paid me a visit in Indiana.

There is a lot of research on the dog heart. I'm speaking of the spiritual heart. There is a shared opinion that a dog will do well, if he is given to a new family and treated kindly. Perhaps if he is young, he would adjust without too much trauma. Aside from that, even a temporary situation, involving a new home, can be devastating. I could site a number of examples, but this one will do. Rachael and her husband Jason had the opportunity to go to Fiji for ten days. Tala was a year old at the time and was very bonded to them. The day they left, they put Tala in the hands of a nice couple who ran a dog sitting service in their home. She was given affection, her favorite food and long walks in the countryside. She was miserable, pacing constantly and not eating well.

I could feel her emotional state and was having a difficult time concentrating on anything, even chocolate. Knowing that was my clue to worry seriously, I called a popular pet psychic on an urge. She connected with Tala, who was not happy with her new family. She was also afraid that the lady was going to be her new mommy. The psychic was able to calm her down, assuring her that it was only a temporary situation while her family was on vacation. The following day, I called the people that Tala was staying with, inquiring about her. They told me how distraught she had been, but that suddenly, she had stopped pacing and began to eat better. They were amazed at her change in behavior and thankful for it.

Animals have souls and when you have souls, you have feelings. We are all part God, part animal, part human, part everything. Think of a rainbow. The most basic description is light, shining through water droplets. Beyond that, it has a magical essence to it, stirring us deeply. It's an image of our souls and our physical bodies. We are all made of light, all seven colors. It is a bridge, connecting the earth and the sky, linking both worlds, and also, acting as a gateway to your highest self. It is God, as the sun, and Goddess, as the water, blending together, using the physical world to reveal themselves, and to remind us that we are light.

"We have forgotten that we belong to each other." Mother Theresa.

CHAPTER TWELVE

SOUL OF THE WILD WOODS

*"To live is so startling, it leaves
little time for anything else."*
Emily Dickenson

Animals. It is a lovely word. A sweet word. A wild word. Animals taste the earth. They bathe in the rain. The silver cheek of the moon, lights their route. They run with the golden staff of the sun, pounding over the hips of the earth, the soft curves of flowering hills and sloping meadows. They dress in their own jewels and sit on their own thrones of tree stumps and boulders, flanked by the fall foliage of maple leaves. They are the heartbeat of the earth, and we disgrace them.

Before I met Shaula Pearl, I met Betsy at a college board meeting. We bonded over donuts and rescue dogs. She invited me out to her ranch where she housed over fifty greyhounds who needed homes. Most of them had retired from the racing business. A few of them had been left at the ranch by their owners who didn't want them anymore.

They were a noisy group, barking up a storm, as we walked along dirt pathways, saying hello to them in their outdoor cages. Betsy stressed the fact that they were not a bunch of ill-mannered dogs, releasing a large greyhound from his cage, proving her right. His name was Bruce. He became immediately passive, walking up to me, slow and dignified. Betsy said to me, "They just want to be heard." I understood that.

Betsy left me with Bruce for a few minutes while she answered her phone. He sat by me, leaning against my legs, not making a sound. I didn't either. It felt good, sharing a quiet moment with him. He seemed shy and a little nervous, but he was glad to be out of his cage, pawing the dirt and wagging his tail slightly. When Betsy returned, she took his leash, letting him walk with us. She showed me a small group, off by themselves, who were considered senior dogs, eight years and up. Many of them had health problems. She commented on how gentle these dogs were, considering the life they had lived.

I didn't know much about greyhounds, so I asked her what she had meant. She had plenty to say. "The racing industry breeds tens of thousands of greyhounds, more than it needs for the racing tracks. Thousands are killed each year who do not breed well, lack racing potential or are injured. They are not euthanized, which would be bad enough. They are hit repeatedly until they are dead, or they are abandoned or starved. Some are lucky enough to retire and given to shelters and animal adoption agencies. Also, during their racing life, they spend most of their adult life in crates or enclosed pens."

She paused, asking me if I wanted the good news. "Please," was all I said, too upset to respond further. She explained how the industry itself is decreasing, and thousands of these beautiful dogs are up for adoption every year. She emphasized the fact that greyhounds make amazing family members and are very gentle and sweet, adjusting to new surroundings easily. She then told me about a close friend who had adopted one of her greyhounds, a gentle girl named Zella. Betsy had warned her friend about their genetic disposition to chase, plus their amazing eyesight. They can see a half mile away. As a result, they should never be off a leash. Also, they can reach forty-five miles per hour in four strides. Her friend had cats, indoors and outdoors. She brought Zella back the next day, because she wouldn't stop chasing them. Fortunately, the greyhound was enchanted. Betsy adopted him.

As the seventh month dawned, I wanted more for her – everything that enchanted puppies had. I ordered blankets with paw prints from gift magazines. I bought her a large purple throw rug in New York and carried it on the plane to the LA airport. I nibbled on her kibble, just to make sure it didn't have a bad after-taste. I bought her stuffed animals in a variety of dog breeds, placing them around the house, hoping that she would pick one she liked and introduce it to her buffalo. A princess should have selections. She ignored them all, choosing the large bag they came home in.

I noticed that her play was different. It was more energetic and confident, batting paper bags around with her paws and ripping them apart for minutes at a time. When she was done with it, she would prance off with a large piece of it in her mouth, her trophy.

It was hard to clean up her joy party. It was shredded evidence that she played hard. She was a glow soul with her paper bags. After one such episode, a neighbor knocked on the door, asking to come in, claiming her phone wasn't working, and she didn't have a land line. I let her in, in spite of the fact that my Hansel and Gretel décor was in full swing. The classic question presented itself "How's Shawna?" I behaved. I didn't care. I was on enchanted overdrive. She didn't stay long, kicking aside a fairly good sized remnant of joy by the front door. She smiled at her foot. Joy is contagious.

At the start of the month, I taught a night class on human development. I began the first lecture with, of course, odd words. "Life, whether it manifests as a human, a Shaula Pearl or a snapdragon, is a cellular miracle. Any questions?" As I anticipated, there was. A young man in the front row raised his hand. He asked me, "What is a Shaula Pearl?" I grinned. I explained that it was my nickname for the word dog. She ended up in many of my lectures. Her various stages of enchantment or development, showed similar growth patterns when it came to humans. In fact, when a new semester started, students would ask me how she was doing.

The class that day, ended with an unusual silence, following these words. "As a general rule, within four weeks, your clump of heart cells, the size of poppy seeds, are motionless. You have no heartbeat, but you are alive. At some preconceived moment, one heart cell jolts, starting a chain reaction. Your heart beats for the first time. At that point, you have barely gone from a blob shape to a kidney bean shape, with your heart, the size of the round red tip at the top of a matchstick. If you lined up embryos, at this stage, from humans to animals, you can't tell them apart. 1.5% of our DNA, makes us human. 75% matches dogs. 33% matches daffodils." Our internal structure connects us to everything. Our outer structure is, in a sense, illusory.

As I was walking to my car, I was stopped by a student. She asked me a question, having nothing to do with human development. It was about dogs. My reputation was spreading. Basically, she had a small dog that was an inside dog. She and husband decided they wanted a large dog to guard their yard. She wanted advise on how to take care of a larger animal. I was stunned, but I didn't show it. I told her that size had nothing to do with anything. All dogs have feelings, the same as humans – babies and grandmothers included. I also told her that all dogs should be family members first. She was a nice lady, and I gave her big points for being concerned.

Shaula Pearl's vanishing acts were increasing. I would come home, and she wouldn't be on the stairs. It's not that she had to be there, but it usually meant she was off on an adventure that didn't support her. One particular night, she was elsewhere. I ruled out the house quickly and then checked the yard, as usual. There was an odd sound near the palm tree, like a broom sweeping rocks. I found her in the ditch, with her head, peering over the wood planks. I joined her, urging her onto high ground, having no idea what spooked her. Once in her closet, she relaxed, curling up with a sock plastered against her belly.

I sat with her, telling her how brave she was, that she didn't scale the fence, that she walked upstairs without a belly hug. As I was leaving, she pawed the rug, once. She was asking me to come back. She wanted my attention. Seven months of worries, fears and unsettling noises, slid down my cheeks. I wiped them off, wanting to use her paw, but I didn't think she would appreciate it. Instead, I wrote her something....The earth is alive. She sings with the wind. She laughs with the daffodils. She cries with the rain. She has a heart of fire and the soul of wild birds.

"Go with your emotions" I said to her, eyeing her paw. "Embrace them like the earth does. Never dismiss them. Master them instead. Feel proud of yourself my sweet girl. It would be highly unusual if you never wanted to hide in a ditch."

By the end of the seventh month, little paw prints of miracles occurred. She didn't twitch when I walked behind her. She didn't leave the room when I dropped something. The trash truck didn't send her into a frenzy. I could walk into a bathroom, and she didn't hide in her closet. Up until this point, she was never truly comfortable with me doing anything except reading or writing. What surprised me, more than anything, was the fact that she followed me. I went downstairs, and she was at my heels. I went in the backyard, and she would beat me there, running through the doggie dog without bashing it with her sides. I went up to my room, and there she was, passing me on the stairs, jumping on her bed. Yes, I was her alpha person, the one who protected her and fed her. I also knew that she loved me and was staying close.

Having to know things, I wondered if she would do it again. She did, but that was it for the evening. Buffalo queens have their options. I went to bed that night, dancing under a full moon, swirling in a flared lace skirt with a tambourine, at least mentally. Life was enchanting. It was about to explode with it.

The eighth month marked a zenith in Shaula Pearl's enchantment plan. Never in my entire life, have I ever seen a soul explode in a deluge of Divine Light. Shaula Pearl claimed the moment. The dog goddess unleashed. Untethered. Fears forgotten. Joy, deep and rich and magical, bleeding to the source, her soul. What she did, leaves me struggling for words. It always will. When you discover your soul and who you are, and you feel it, and you believe it, you can't describe it in words. The moment is too powerful. It has nowhere to go but outward. Even today, it stops me in my tracks. Her joy. Her joy run.

It manifested one night, close to midnight, while I was sitting on the floor, in my bedroom, giving myself a private reading with an oracle deck. The power card leapt out, landing on my lap. It was a great reminder that true power, ever-lasting power, comes from within, not without, the moment of birth. Every soul is a baby goddess, gurgling in full potential. My thoughts drifted, enjoying the message and the calm tides of the evening.

I fanned out the remainder of the cards, planning on extending the reading. Shaula Pearl pranced in, stopping directly in front of me. She froze, staring at me with the intensity of a bon fire. "What's up?" I said, always happy to see her and wondering if my oracle deck was about to get shredded. She pawed the rug like a bull, waiting for the gate to open. It did, deep inside of her, and she blasted out of it, thundering down the hallway in a wild and fearless explosion of raw joy.

My jaw dropped, literally. She flew down the stairs, woofing. It's a deeper and more primal bark. I gave me the chills. I ran to the hallway, leaning over the banister, watching for blackbirds. Maybe a family had flown in through the doggie door. Maybe there was a bunny orb on the couch. I wasn't getting it. She was racing around the living room, snorting and barking now, and without warning, pounded up the stairs like a herd of cows. I ran into the bedroom, afraid that she would knock me over. I threw myself into the swivel chair, as wide-eyed as she was. She flew over the New York throw rug, twisting in mid-air over my oracle deck and landing briefly on the bed. One second later, she was hurtling down the hall, barking.

She wasn't done. She paused at the top of the stairs, and with one mighty huff, she took off for a second round, barking and thundering all over the house like a wild, feral animal. She was back in the bedroom within minutes, panting heavily but grinning a mile wide. Once you feel joy, you can't get enough of it. She blasted out of the room, one more time, jumping on her bed, snorting. Then, she came galloping into my room, leaping onto the bed. I caught her expression as she came flying in. She was moving too fast to catch anything else, except her tail.

She stopped. It was over, for the moment. My bed was trampled with joy, and I was sure the house was. It didn't matter. Nothing mattered. All I could manage to say was, "You felt it, didn't you." Tears were coming, clogging my throat. I had witnessed the birth of joy, in all of its glory. A spontaneous combustion of Divine Light. The fires of wild woods, burning in her soul - uncontainable. Unquenched.

She was enchanted.

Sleep was miles away. Her joy run had shocked me beyond words, beyond anything. It also had left me wired. I tried the chakra meditation, hoping to relax, but when I got to the yellow, all I could think of was sunflowers bursting with light. I tried yoga breathing, deep and raspy, but I sounded more like I was choking. I focused on one large dot, flashing a bright white, but it reminded me of her body, skyrocketing around the house in full goddess mode. Finally, I drifted off to a sweet dream. Sugar plum puppies, all frosted and sparkly, were swirling around the cosmos in full control of their lives, with little joy buttons attached to their paws. I smiled in my dream. Shaula Pearl would be in my head, forever.

After that, joy runs began stacking up. Many of them manifested when I was writing, but her most dramatic joy runs took place the moment I went to bed....She feels the magic of her ageless soul, and without pain and sadness, she is free and fearless. Sometimes, I run with her, closing my eyes, flying inches above her back, barely touching her. I can see her paws igniting and her peacock feather, bobbing in a smooth gait, glowing like moonlight. Her eyes are fire opals. She breathes heavily, hammering in air, hurtling over blue-green ponds and hidden pathways of lavender and sage, journeying deep. She rides her soul, remembering all that she is.

What I love most about them, besides the joy factor, is her freedom of movement, the wildness of it, the power of it. We lose it, in a sense, as we grow older. Toddlers can throw themselves into outdoor fountains or skip down the aisles of a market and be tagged normal. Those who are labeled old, fight the illusion of it, dancing on the beach, twirling long scarves and floppy hats. They get away with it. Those of us who are somewhere in the middle, have lost the freedom to move without social biases. If I ran down the mall, giggling, I would meet the security guards.

Everyone has the right to a joy run. Joy rights. It doesn't matter who you are or what specie you are. In truth, my favorite part is the moment before it begins. I can see it in her eyes. Behind her eyes. It's a magical place where she feels the expansion of her own soul, beyond the perimeters of her body. It is the moment before dawn breaks.

Pooh understood. "Although eating honey was a very good thing to do, there was a moment just before you began to eat it, which was better than when you were. But he didn't know what it was called."

CHAPTER THIRTEEN

PLUSH DREAMS

"I would rather sit on a pumpkin,
and have it all to myself,
Than to be crowded on a velvet cushion."
Henry David Thoreau

Nine months in. I had help besides my incredible support team of angels, dog angels and the ponderings of pooh bear. I had tools. I knew the importance of them, their usefulness and their feel good elements. I love my apple green ladder. It lessens the drudgery of lugging it around the house, changing light bulbs in ceiling fans. I love my toaster. Its whimsical, covered in bright colorful ladybugs. I drink out of a gold and purple chalice when I write, a goddess thing. I didn't want anything less for Shaula Pearl, in any area of her life, including dog accessories.

You don't have to purchase the most expensive or the most ornate to enchant a soul. Use whatever resources you already have. Your house is full of them. Look in your kitchen, your closets, your garage and under your bed. Socks, old gift bags, worn t-shirts and boxes can enchant as much as a twenty dollar accordion crocodile stuffed with crinkly material. She does love her buffalo, but you can find an enchanted stuffed animal in a thrift store.

I took everything, involving her well-being, as important. The right to the perfect brush is critical to being a goddess. Mine has to be purple with tipped bristles. It has to be in the same place every morning, so I don't lose it. It has clout. My comb and nail clippers are thrown into a drawer. Shaula Pearl has clout. She deserved the most flawless and enchanting hair brush I could find. The challenge began. I brought her home two hair brushes, wanting her opinion. Stainless steel pins made her cringe. Stiff bristles didn't do it either, leaving her huffing out of the bedroom. I went back to the store in full and unwavering focus, determined to leave angels out of it. Asking for a hair brush angel didn't seem respectful. I gave in, and there it was - the perfect choice. It was a boar bristle brush, crème colored with a wooden handle.

Shaula Pearl said yes, standing a little rigid for the most part, but she allowed me to brush her for the first time. Her head lowered slowly, with a small poof of air whooshing out of her mouth. She was feeling it. After less than a minute, she was done, running to her closet. I never question her. She was finished with it and that was that.

When it comes to beds, I sleep in trees. My headboard and frame are wood. When it came to Shaula Pearl's bed, I bought her an orthopedic dog bed lined with pink, matching the spot on her nose. Her dog bowls are plastic microban bowls that have a large width to them, making them tip resistant. They were a new find. But what I love most, are her assortment of blankets. She plays with them like a child, discovering something magic in the mundane. If this isn't a pose of enchantment, I don't know what is.

We have a love affair with food. We emotionally respond to it. I eat German chocolate cake on my mother's birthday and coffee cake on my father's birthday. Food makes lasting memories. After an intense night of trick or treating, the trading would begin. It was never fair. My brother and sister knew that I was a fool for butterfingers.

Animals love their food, also. They need their vitamins and minerals, and they have to break down their food to make fuel, just like humans. One big difference is our metabolism. We need more energy than a sloth. One big similarity is, we both have individual taste buds. Mesa loved crunch so she ate carrots and all kinds of raw vegetables. It took me a few months to find a kibble that Wicca liked. Neither dog would touch a banana.

Being an enchantress, I hold the magic wand. Food needed to be part of the plan. High quality food was important, enchanting her insides. I kept her away from grains such as corn and wheat, knowing that she already had a sensitive stomach. I shunned the word byproducts. It slithers off the tongue, hiding itself in the majority of our dry and wet dog food. Millions of dead animals, from road damage to kill shelters, make up some of the bulk in our beautifully designed dog food bags with picturesque mountain peaks and sprawling meadows. Hair, teeth, beaks, heads and organs, are crushed and mixed in with the remaining ingredients. Since they are not digestible, they turn into sugar, causing nervous energy. One out of four dogs, die of cancer every year. In my opinion, we feed them cancer.

Also, I made sure that I didn't leave any common household food items within reach, toxic to dogs. The most common ones to avoid are avocados, baby food, dairy products, fat trimmings, raw eggs, grapes, raisins, nuts, potato peels and tomatoes. Take a breath. Add cat food. As a rule, it's too high in protein for a dog's stomach, requiring more fiber. Shaula Pearl was such a selective eater, I wasn't worried that she would raid the refrigerator, although one night, she surprised me. I left a plate of food on the kitchen counter and went upstairs, searching for my phone. She ate half a sweet potato, half a paper plate and my cherry tomatoes had dents in them, with the addition of one white glow hair. I ate toast that evening.

I had more help. Homeopathic enchantment made a difference. Rescue Remedy, a natural blend of five different flowers, sold in many health stores for human consumption, is a great product. It calms behavior, reducing stress, so I put a few drops in her dog food. Chamomile tea is great for relieving anxiety in humans and dogs. Mixing a little warm tea with her breakfast, helped lessen her panic attacks. Lavender oil works like magic. It almost sedates you. I rubbed some along the rim of her food bowl and sometimes on her paws. Once in a while, I rubbed a few drops of it on my arm where she sniffs. It calms the central nervous system. Always ask your vet if a certain food product or homeopathic product would be a good idea for your dog. What works for Shaula Pearl, might not be the right choice for you and your enchanting animal.

Besides the food factor, massage can be a wonderful experience for dogs. When Wicca was dying of cancer, I had a friend massage her, using her Reike abilities, a Japanese holistic system of energy healing. It's very gentle and noninvasive, especially if your dog is experiencing pain or anxiety. You can also follow various hand positions in a book. A good overall method is to place one hand on the top of the head and the other hand below the jaw. Slowly move both hands along the body, ending at the tail bone. This type of massage or healing, helps with health issues and emotional trauma.

We are radiantly electrical. Our energy source is chemical. Our brain generates enough watts of energy to power up a light bulb. In fact, everything is made of energy, with a variety of frequencies, even chocolate. Raw chocolate is a high vibrational food with its enchanting antioxidants. I feel safe and happy when I consume chocolate. My energy field glows. People can feel it. I'm sure that Shaula Pearl feels it, so eating a fair amount is certainly in her best interest. Healthy dog food has high vibrations, also – more life force.

Sound, in particular, has certain frequencies that accelerate healing. Music therapy for dogs has become popular in veterinary hospitals and shelters, reducing the stress of trauma and anxiety. Internal organs slow down with certain vibrations. Arthritic dogs fall asleep faster. Wicca listened to music designed for animals, helping her feel calm, during her last few weeks. Now, I play similar music for Shaula Pearl, relaxing her instantly. It works like a charm.

Touch. Sound. Vibrations. Language. These are all tools of enchantment. But your words are perhaps the most miraculous. I walked into a small café recently, giving my order to a young girl who didn't look at me. It feels abnormal to have human interaction without eye contact, but I shrugged it off, paying her and thinking about her hair color. It was a luminous shade of purple. I wanted it. Without any preconceived notion of enchanting anyone, I said to her, "I love your hair." You would have thought it rained diamonds, right there where she was standing. Her entire expression shape shifted. It glowed. Her eyes sparkled. Her earrings jangled. Her spine straightened. She smiled, thanking me. I smiled back, feeling her good vibes. As a committed enchantress, I made a promise that day. I would generously pay back the universe for everything I had, and if I didn't have much, I had words.

Shaula Pearl thrives on words, being ultra-sensitive to the sound of them. When I speak to her, I use my authentic voice, my normal voice, so she's familiar with it. Sometimes, I speak to her in a special language called Parentese, now deemed one of the most positive approaches to parenting by early childhood specialists. To me, it's love talk. You elongate sounds. You speak in a higher pitch, a sing-song sound. It grabs the attention of young minds and animals. For example, you might say, "Your paws are sooooo sweet, like cinnamon rolls." It doesn't matter what you say, it is the sound of what you say. Shaula Pearl gets all gooey eyed when I speak Parentese. Her lower jaw vibrates. Her entire body goes limp, slowly and dreamily, melting onto the carpet like she is drugged. May we all be euphoric on love energy.

Life is alive with magical things, imploring us to move gently, to listen to the sound of our own breathing, to feel the world like the woods do. Pine trees with their dark brown bark, cracked by time, whisper of sun hungry skies and dark moons churning the cycles of our immortal origins. They know their roots, twisting like giant wood snakes, holding their world together. A lusty, loud-mouthed toad burrows under them, hiding himself, hearing our thunderous complaints about the way the world is. He looks around, rich in damp soil, wondering what all the fuss is about. A grey owl glides quietly, tasting the night air scented with wild raspberries. He wonders, also.

I saved my favorite enchanting assistant for last. Her name is Magda Gerber. She passed away in 2007 but left us with amazing methods to enchant the young souls of infants and toddlers, all dog friendly. She focused on respectful care, treating children like a whole person, a unique individual with real feelings. I love that. Some people view the very young or the very old as if they are less than human, with meaningless things to say. Animals are often seen in that same misguided light.

Magda believed that young children would develop strong self-esteem, by playing undisturbed, making their own discoveries, and not being asked to do things they weren't ready for. Most importantly, she believed that babies are complete individuals, with their own set of needs and emotions – the baby goddess. Also, you should talk directly to them, not over them, and at all times, tell them what you are doing. I'm changing your diapers. I'm lifting your leg. I'm kissing your paw.

I use many of her methods with Shaula Pearl. I talk to her constantly, telling her what I'm doing, when I'm getting up, what I'm making for dinner. I try to see the world through her eyes. What does my broom look like? It's doesn't have arms or legs, but it has a wild, bushy head. The large gift bag on my bed, with lotions and perfumes, is a hostile creature with odd odors. The opened drawer, sticking out of my tall dresser, is something new and dangerous, not to be trusted.

Magda's philosophy is based on trust and respect. I focused on those words, creating my own list of suggestions for living with an abused animal. Hence, the eight step enchantment list.

 Number One: Create an environment that is mentally nourishing. Have open pathways for moving about freely. Decrease loud noises and soften lights. Collect matches.

Number Two: Nurture the inner-directed Goddess. Allow for exploring with a flair for individual needs. Have a closet available. Never demand anything. Suggest. Do you want a sock or a buffalo, or both?

Number Three: Make sensitive observations. Care enough to notice what your dog is doing or not doing. Adjust the environment as needed. Hide nice throw pillows. Add washable throw rugs.

Number Four: Quality time is all the time. Never be too busy to stop what you're doing and show affection. Family first. Family forever. Give while your hand is warm and alive.

Number Five: You are not alone. Involve. If you sit in the sun, invite others to sit with you. Say hello and goodbye. Share your toast.

Number Six: Be a model of consistency, the power of dependability. The test of the stubbed toe. Don't yell and scare anyone. Be gently wounded.

Number Seven: Be a passionate advocate for love. Love in large increments of time. Love always and without conditions. Love when it's easy, when it's hard. Just love.

Number Eight: Live like you are walking a desert. Thirst for nothing but joy. When you find it, share it.

Merging with a soul, on the physical plane, is a beautiful experience. In the case of an abused animal, it will transform you, calling in cosmic waterfalls of divine light, even healing yourself. It can also be an emotional shredder, but it's worth the shred. Many times, I had quick snippets of images portraying her life. She was cold and hungry. Shivering. Terrified. Legs limp. Head bowed. Bones aching. The scent of fear and death, inside and outside of her. And the cries, silent and haunting. I have to remind myself to think beautiful thoughts. Glow feathers. Enchanted paws. Thunderous joy runs. Those are the healing thoughts.

Shaula Pearl has changed me, improved me, given me x-ray vision. I can see vines blossoming in her soul, lacing around her pain, perfuming them with enchantment, with love energy. She has increased my sensitivity to sound. I can hear a snuff, ten yards away. She expanded my soul. I can look at her face and feel the presence of cherubs. Her entire expression has told me things. Streamline. Carve it all down to love. Don't worry so much. Your microwaves dies. You can't find your massacre. You forget something at the market. It doesn't matter in the long run. God and Goddess, Mother and Father, gave you a soul and the power to be yourself and to be strong and magical.

The tenth and eleventh months weaved together on a spinning wheel, creating a rich, thick, golden tapestry of joy, which Shaula Pearl threw herself into constantly. Joy is personal, so give it your own splash of color. People would assume, and rightly so, that my joy color is purple. It was until I met Shaula Pearl. She has a golden glow about her. Gold is valuable, the worth of your soul. It is the love of your soul. When she is off on a run, gold dust scatters in her wake, the spiritual pureness of who she is. If my house is full of something, it is glow hair and gold dust.

Her joy runs are too numerous to count, beginning somewhere in my room and ending behind my swivel chair. She runs with her higher self, feeling her perfected soul in full power. How amazing it would be, if we could joy run through all the moments of our lives. Nothing would scare us. We would name our path, claiming it instantly. There would be nothing we couldn't do. In reality, nothing keeps us from the desires of our heart, except our own fears. They are the great masters of illusion, deceiving us with their flawed guidance.

Soul magic. Love magic. Joy magic. The three sisters of enchantment, strong and seductive, lusting after joy, know their power. They hold hands high in the air, dancing in circles, celebrating the souls who discover them. Not everyone does....Once upon a time, there was a man who had a large dog. He kept the dog in his backyard. The dog barked all the time. No one blamed him. No one ever came out to play. He was alone and sad, knowing how much he had to give. Eventually, he stopped eating. He was thin and wasting away. His ribs looked massive on his withered body. A kindly soul, in the same kingdom, noticed him and called the authorities. They came bearing important news for the owner. If he didn't attend to his needs, they would come back and take his dog. The owner put the dog in his car, with the intention of taking him to the vet, but the dog died on the way there. The owner admitted that his dog had cancer. He had his own perspective on it. Why pay attention to him? Why treat him? He was dying anyways.

Joy run, Shaula Pearl. Do it for yourself, for the dog in the neighborhood who died in the car. Do it for all souls who need love and joy. Do it now.

CHAPTER FOURTEEN

LOVE SPIRITED

*"Yesterday is ashes. Tomorrow is greenwood.
Only today does the fire burn brightly."*
Eskimo Proverb

Without our dreams, life would be flat and colorless. Frozen. With dreams, the deep and poetic longings of our soul, we can have clusters of violets at our feet, peach snapdragons in our garden, or anything we desire. They birth the future, pushing us forward, grinning and exhausted, believing in the brilliance of ourselves, in the magic of the divine mantra - dreams are things you already have and already have become.

One year later.

I dreamed about her before I met her. After we met, I had dreams I wanted to give her. When I brought her home, dreams dripped slowly into the physical world of my home, spinning their enchantment. Not the night dreams, but the day dreams, sculpting our journey, moment to moment. I believed in what we had both wanted – Love. Here it is, a year later but not without changes or surprises. I didn't dream of new décor. I didn't imagine that my new dog would glow in the moonlight. I learned an entirely new language of snuffs and gurgles. I became submerged in thunderous love energy. I loved her when I saw her, but I am not ashamed to say, how deeply I love her now – a dog. A soul. Love for anything should be deep, rich and expressive.

The year has left me a full supporter and believer in the power of enchantment, of love and joy. It is the birthright of all souls. We should seek after it, find it and then spread it around with a luscious wildness to it, like chocolate frosting on a layer cake, in great swirls and wave-like impressions. Shaula Pearl is a prime example. When she is happy, she explodes with it. When she wants my attention, she paws my side until I stop writing. I swivel around in my chair and say, "What?" It's an inside joke. When she is outside, romping through the flowering weeds, she stops to sniff a dandelion or a peppermint leaf, wagging her tail now. Still, if she is startled, she runs to her closet. We all run somewhere.

"The cat will mew, and dog will have his day." Shakespeare was feeling it. These are her days now. She is sweet and gentle with a vibrant energy about her. She is tirelessly dogged when she wants something, mainly a belly rub, but she goes about it with the grace of a true princess. She barks softly at me, wanting my hand. My foot doesn't count, according to her. I tried it once, deep into a paragraph, stretching my leg out, rubbing her belly with my foot. She left the room. Also, her biscuit amuses her like a friend. She won't eat it, right away. Instead, she stares at it, playing with it a little, batting it with a paw – her inner cat. I will never tire of her enchantment.

She demonstrates intellect on many levels. I think about washing my hair, and she runs outside. It doesn't matter what day it is. She knows things. She doesn't mess on the carpet as much, but when she does, she stays upstairs. When I enter the house, she peeks at me between the guard rails. I've never yelled at her for doing anything, but she knows I have my opinions. If it's Saturday, and I'm sleeping in, she checks on me. She barks once near my head. I wake up and tell her that I'm okay. She doesn't wake me again, even if I sleep late.

She is also charming and clever. If I'm staring at my laptop, way too long, I know what my needs are - a real, live, electrical body. I need to look in her exceptionally sweet eyes, where love pools. Where the meaning of life glows in a dog's eye. Then I yell, with a soft edge to it, "Where's my girl?" She prances down the hall, nudges me and goes back to her room. She knows what her needs are. When the mood hits, she likes to be alone. Sometimes, I type in the dark, losing myself in words– my lamp, long forgotten. She sneaks up on me, throwing a sock at my feet. If I don't notice it, she barks once and runs out of the room. Once, she looked at her water bowl and then back at me and back at the water bowl. I didn't blame her, now that she's a princess. There was a huge water bug in it, flapping around. "Oh, I see," I said, rescuing it. "Your water is a no swim zone."

Did I mention fearless? She tries new things even it takes her a year. I was sitting on the bed, reading a book that kept slipping out of my hands. It's pointless to read when you're asleep. I turned off a small lamp within reach, expecting her to bolt off, running out of the room. This time, she didn't. She sat with me. Of course, my nose itched like it was falling off. I was afraid to move my arm. I also wanted to sneeze, so I banged my tongue up against the roof of my mouth, hoping to stall it. I was afraid to move anything. It was another magical moment, even if it didn't last long. Thirty seconds and she was off. The bed is elevated for the alpha person. She doesn't understand that I would be joyfully okay with it.

The first year created a new social agenda — girls night out with the courageous pizza eating wonder dog. My friends have become accustomed to her charming ways. Lights are low. Our demented desires to have a scream fest, on hold. The pizza appears at the door, hot and steamy and passed around quickly. Shaula Pearl comes downstairs, fixated on the scent. She stands motionless, looking at me and the pizza, me and the pizza. I don't let her wait long. I say to her, "Go get it." She makes her move, politely eating a small slice of it on her own personal paper plate. When she's done, she sits on the stairs, watching us make fools of ourselves. If someone she doesn't know, happens to be in the living room, she looks at me and the pizza and then runs to her closet. Fear is so crippling.

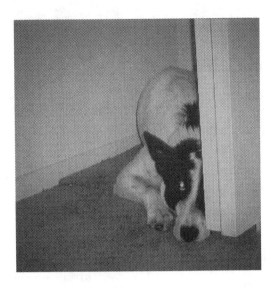

Food is still an odd issue with her. She loves toast, pasta, rice, and cheese. She doesn't like much of anything else, except her dog food. If I place something new under her nose, she sniffs once and strolls away, aware that she has choices. If it doesn't feel right, she doesn't do it. That is a goddess thing. I might try again, convinced that she will go dog wild over it. The 'I' again. Sometimes, she eats it. Other times, she carries it off in her mouth, only to please me. I might find it in another part of the house, sometimes under my foot.

She never barks for a treat. When I'm in the kitchen, she sits in the living room with that look. How can you resist a staring and enchanted dog who might be a cat? I put a biscuit by her paw. She ignores it. When I leave the kitchen, she picks it up, prances by me on the stairs and waits for me in my bedroom. When I sit at my desk, she eats it.

She does things that truly amaze me. In the morning, I sit on my prayer rug, either praying or meditating. The moment I begin, she comes into the room, sitting directly in front of me, inches from my face. She doesn't move until I'm done. She joins me. Your dog will rise to the connection that you make together. You take the lead. You form the relationship.

If you live alone, it is you and your dog, with limitless opportunities to share toast, to have conversations about sea-dragons or dog biscuits. It doesn't matter what you talk about, as long as you talk. If you treat your dog like he's invisible, he will be. If you think of him as a lower life form, with no disrespect to the worm, then your dog will act worm, wandering around your house, looking for decomposed food and not much else. Your dog will have little understanding of who you are and what you need. He won't help you become a better human. He is ready to love you. He is so divinely kindhearted. Yell at me, and I forgive you. Forget to feed me, and I wait. Leave me alone in the backyard, and I miss you. Leave me alone for a long time, and I wither with sadness. You are my pack, and I am being dismissed and forgotten.

One of the most endearing things that she does, occurs in the morning, while I'm still in bed, and sometimes, while I'm asleep. She stands on her hind legs, resting her head on the mattress. She scared me the first time it happened. I woke up, with her nose, an inch from my nose. I couldn't figure it out, until I sat up. The enchanted moment was broken, but she does it often enough.

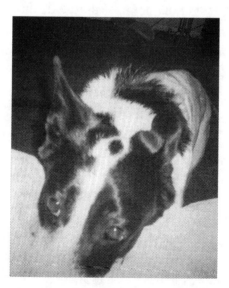

Our language creates our reality, the very landscape we walk on. Still, words are odd to me. An apple is only an apple, because we gave it the name apple. In reality, it's an edible fruit. It could have labeled, Godzilla. I was at workshop recently, focusing on animals and their ability to understand speech. I shared the owl lady's suggestion about leaving the house and using the same words, which I do, even today. The last thing I say, before I shut the front door, is -"I'll be back."

A lady in the audience made the following comment. "Dogs don't understand the word 'back.' I agreed with her to an extent. If you looked at your dog and said the word back, it wouldn't mean anything. If you said the word back and raised a paw, it would mean a handshake. Shaula Pearl associates the word back, with me, returning to the house. The sound of the word and what follows, gives it meaning.

The combination of sounds can be a fun learning tool, not only for dogs but for children. Adjectives make language luscious and rich. Would you like a juicy orange? A sweet and smooth piece of chocolate? I experimented with language, placing a chewy dog treat on a paper plate and a crunchy one on a plate next to it. I picked up the chewy one, held it under her nose and said, chewy. I did the same thing with the second bone, saying crunchy. For three nights in a row, she ate the crunchy one. After that, she would drool if I said the word crunchy. Interaction creates intelligence. It's nothing brainy. Dogs love it when you do anything with them.

We have a talking relationship. If we didn't, she wouldn't understand human language, as well as she does. If I'm cold in the morning, I roll out of bed muttering, "I'm going downstairs to turn up the heat. I'm not feeding us yet." She stares at me with her eyes half closed. If I say, "Time for breakfast," she follows me. If I go downstairs, late in the evening, I say to her, "No more eating for us, girl." She closes her eyes, ignoring me. If I don't say anything, she runs down with me, eyes wide open and her big tail, swiping the guardrails like a feather duster.

Besides language, the best enchantment supporters are freebees. We play games. I'm typing as usual, pretending that I don't have to eat or sleep. She sits behind me, barks once and rolls over on her back. If I rub her belly, with my hand, she doesn't move. If I rub her belly with my foot, she doesn't leave me anymore. She gets this weird look in her eyes, jumps up and goes on a joy run. There is also the paper wad game, with me as the mad writer, scrunching up paper and tossing them over my shoulder, grunting. She loves it. She pounces on them, joyously shredding my ideas.

I've come to accept the fact that her history is a mystery. Lack of early socialization would be the reason for many of her habits. She won't lick you on the face. She won't chase something and bring it back to you. She won't rough and tumble with you. She doesn't have any spatial awareness between herself and whatever I'm doing. If she's blocking my way, she doesn't move, so I walk around her. If I try to move her, she becomes hard as stone. She also informs me about where she's been, nudging me on the side. If she's warm, I know she's been sitting in the sun. If she's cold, she's been glowing under the moon. She involves me in her life. That was modeled.

Joy runs still occur without warning. If I light candles and dim lights, she goes for it. If I rest for a minute, stretching out like a cat on the bed, she's off. Also, she goes into the ditch for more pleasurable reasons than hiding. She digs and plunges around, throwing dirt and leaves in the air. She enjoys sitting on the wood planks, calm and confident like an Egyptian goddess with a peacock headdress.

One of the very first pictures that I took of her, reflects a rigid and frightened soul, who was afraid to be in the yard. You can tell how different she feels now, by looking at the two photos.

If joy runs ushered in the first half of the year, Divine Light came pouring in at the end. It was an ordinary night, full of the normal oddities. I spilt soda on my desk. There was a strange sound downstairs, and I noticed her comforter, usually on her bed, halfway into the hall. Buffalo was in my room, and I had no clue where any of my socks were.

I was writing and baking brownies at the same time – my version of multi-tasking. Shaula Pearl was sitting in the hallway, darting her head back and forth, watching something. It often precedes a joy run. Instead, she pranced in, poking me in the side. Usually, this would have not prompted a picture, but for some reason, I grabbed my camera. A column of white light, directly behind me, was surrounding her, almost completely. Divine Light loves our animals.

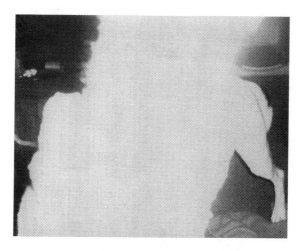

I live in a house with a dog who has given me a wide variety of décor. Creative expression should never be repressed. She has also given me a clear glimpse of her soul, that is so incredibly sweet and unique, that I feel honored. Blessed? Yes, more than I ever have. Shaula Pearl has been one of my greatest teachers in the field of absolute love, the main module of the angelic realms. Love is the religion. Love is the kingdom.

God spelled backwards is, of course, dog. I don't think it's a fluke. I think it's a message. Dogs are the divine energies of love and light, the very countenance of God and Goddess, glowing within them. They just love, and they want us to love back without a reason, without a condition. They don't care about our human flaws, and they don't judge us by them. They see the unblemished rose, not any of its raggedy petals frayed by the wind. They see beauty in us. They see God in us. They want us to see God in each other.

CHAPTER FIFTEEN

FABULOUS AND FOREVER

"Be not the slave of your past.
Plunge into the sublime seas,
dive deep and swim far, so you shall
come back with new power."
Ralph Waldo Emerson

Five years later.

Lights are out. Candles are lit. There is a warm amber blush to the bedroom with a slight scent of cinnamon. Tall shadows dance dreamily on the walls to the languid movement of candle flames – their hot fiery souls, oblivious to my fingers, pecking at the keyboard like hungry birds. Everything is connected but flourishing in its own moment.

Shaula Pearl, sitting by me, has a pale golden glow about her. I think she is part chameleon, absorbing colors. She's watching my hands. I know what's coming. She barks once, shifting her eyes to my face. I pause, rubbing the top of her head slowly, circling around her peacock feather. She likes that. Her eyes get all glassy and distant, perhaps looking into other worlds. I look at her sweet face, perfectly enchanted. She is the heart of my chewed up home. I nod, smiling at her, knowing how things that you thought you cherished, pale in importance, when you stack them next to a soul who is as lovely as the magnolia blossoms in your front yard.

I kiss her nose on the pink spot. She doesn't flinch, allowing me this pleasure. A moment later, she prances out of the room, without an explanation, planting herself at the top of the stairs, watching something, as usual, that I can't always see. I walk around her, thudding downstairs, wondering if I should prance more. She follows me, waiting for me, a few yards from the kitchen while I grab a soda.

How wonderful it must feel to have choices, to have places where you can just be and nobody bothers you or wants you to explain yourself.

She follows me upstairs, sitting behind my chair, staring at me. She barks once, flopping on her side, asking for a belly rub. Her wish is granted, of course, but I stop to scratch my nose. She paws at me, knowing that her paw has power. 'Time for bed," I announce, a few minutes later, admitting that I need to sleep and knowing that I would have to be the one suggesting it. She understands, prancing down the hall, jumping on her bed. Within the hour, she comes back in, lying at the side of my bed. She sleeps by me now.

I lie in bed, listening. It's a forever habit. The room is robed in darkness, except for one small candle fighting for its life. I refuse to get up and blow it out. Joy to light. Joy to the night where Shaula Pearl curls up, safe and warm with her buffalo, a little scruffy. She still sleeps with her eyes partially open, remembering the fear. But now, she knows that she is safe and cared for. Valued. Respected. Afraid of it ending. Afraid of losing what she has. That's what I sense, now.

Going outside on a walk is not going to happen. I open the front door, looking at her, raising an eyebrow, tap dancing a little. She steps back and then runs upstairs, fear nipping at her heels. Her boundaries are set in cement. I can relate to that. Don't touch my hair if you don't know me. Don't feed me milk chocolate. I won't eat an animal if it has a face. I overlook fish. They look at you sideways. It's half a face. I feel guilty about it, but not enough, evidently. I will admit though, at one point in my life, the promise of duck in orange sauce was a justifiable reason for accepting a date.

She snuffs and wheezes a little, but gurgling is gone for the most part. I miss it. Gone is the one-dog demolition team on the house. I don't miss that. Also, she barks less on a joy run. Rubbing her belly still prompts a bark and so will the front door, as I open it. One bark for everything. She never strings them out. Recently, she made two new sounds. One of them is kind of a gruff-a-hump. She makes it when she's moving around the house, exploring and sniffing. Then, she'll stop, pawing at nothing, with a wild look in her eyes. She's playing, cracking herself up. The other sound scares me, only because she does it behind me, quickly, knowing that I can sense her. It sounds like a loud yawn ending with a screech. The last time she did it, I jerked my arm, knocking over a small candle on my desk, spilling wax everywhere. She ran down the hall, grabbed buffalo and pretended like nothing happened. She owed me a picture.

She rarely goes into the yard without me, so I sit on the wood planks, a few times a day when I'm home, if only to get her outside. She meanders around the yard, finding warm spots and sitting in them. She moves frequently. I don't think she has a plan. She moves to move. You can't move in a packed cage. Recently, I was eating a bowl of cereal on the wood planks. Shaula Pearl came over, resting by me, putting her head on my leg. She's never done that. I was afraid to eat, that it would break that enchanted moment. It was hard. My Crispi's were chanting in soy milk, luring me in. I folded. I took one small bite. She lifted her head, but that was it. The snapping and popping medley must be agreeable to her.

She still loves to go in the ditch, playing in it about as wild as she gets. Sometimes, I sneak over, wanting to watch all the unbridled joy.

If I get too close, she stops, moves out of the ditch and sits in the yard. At least, she doesn't bolt into the house anymore. At the same time, sounds are still very disturbing to her - a loud voice over the fence or outdoor machinery makes her bolt, and if a crow flying overhead, caws loudly, she's gone.

Living with Shaula Pearl has made me appreciate moments. I was caught in a sudden rainstorm with my two year old granddaughter, Scarlet. We didn't scream or run for cover. We looked up, tasting the rain. We grinned after that, sharing one of those moments that fly by way too fast but stay with you forever. Scarlet said, "I love the rain. This is crazy!" I told her that I did too, and that I loved crazy. I suggested that we love it at her friend's house, a few blocks away. There are times when getting soaked in a moment, needs your discernment.

Also, I move with more mindful intention, feeling more alive and aware of myself. Life is richer and more detailed. It elongates the day. I twist doorknobs slower, the ones that are left. I walk to my car, instead of half-galloping. I put the lid on a peanut butter jar tightly, instead of leaving it half screwed on. I suck on chocolate. I chew toast slower. I remember eating it.

I see the world close up, twinkling with color and design – the silvery threads in licorice grass, near my house, and the dark chocolate specks on tiger lilies. I notice leaves and their shades of green, and if you hold them up toward the sun, you can see thin red lines and pale splashes of yellow in them.

Thank you, Shaula Pearl. She taught me to slow down. She moves leisurely throughout the house, sniffing corners, socks and blankets. She follows me around quietly, sitting when I pause, looking around at things. She lies down with buffalo, unhurriedly, as though her muscles are made of molasses. Her hind legs shake when she gets up. I worry about her more, being twelve now. I tell her that she is a dog goddess and that only her body has an earth age, not her soul. We will joy run together, now and forever.

I attended a psychic fair, with no intention of talking to anyone about Shaula Pearl, which was hard to do. I wanted to zero in on some financial issues, like having enough money for high fiber toast and gourmet dog biscuits. I looked around for a lady who always had positive feedback about the future of my food pantry. She wasn't there, so I requested angelic guidance on who to speak to. I saw an empty chair by a nice looking young man who had purple candles on his table. That was a point, but I was drawn to him because he grinned at me. A good grin was my life now.

Jamie explained his skills, focusing on his ability to connect with animal souls. He further explained that we are all born with this ability, but we push it back and ignore it for many reasons. He mentioned that animals are natural masters of their own intuitive language, having the ability to speak to each other mentally. Point for animals. I was liking him even more. It felt right, asking him about Shaula Pearl. Jamie had a message for me that I will never tire of hearing. He said, "You're dog loves you so much. You saved her life." I was overwhelmed with his comment. Loving me was not a condition, but it was so welcomed.

Jamie then told me that Shaula Pearl had something to say to me, directly. He used her words. "When I get sick, don't call a doctor or give me medicine. Let me rest in my closet. I want to pass over without help."

He asked me if I understood her message. I couldn't speak. All I could do was nod my head, my eyes tearing up. He asked me if I was okay. I told him, "Yes. She fought her fears in her closet. She feels safe there with her sock and her buffalo."

Jamie had one more comment, telling me how protected she was. A few questions followed. "Hasn't she always been healthy? Do her ears ever need cleaning? Does she have an odor about her? How are her eyes? Do they look clear?

It did seem a little odd. Her ears are always clean. Her hair is always soft and smooth, and she smells good. She has a slight, sweet aroma to her like freshly baked cookies. Also, up until the fifth year, there was a thick, red lining at the bottom of her eye, maybe an injury. It looks better now. I'm convinced that she has her own team of animal medics, from the other side, handling her health issues, including her teeth and toenails. I tried clipping them, but she would pant and gurgle. I don't touch them anymore, and they don't grow.

As my ten minutes ended, I asked Jamie to please tell Shaula Pearl that she was a dog goddess and that I was a human goddess and our souls were divine. We would never be separated. He told me that she was aware of that now, that you tell her often enough.

I had no idea how diverse and defined pacing was. She patrols the upstairs hallway, with a serious and clipped pace, when someone knocks on the door. She strolls back and forth, slowly, when she wants me to follow her. When a loud noise frightens her, she paces with more of a heaviness, a thunder pace. Also, there is the melt-down pace, but it's not as bad as it sounds. She paces at a steady gait, from my room to her room, and then stops behind me, poking me. Sometimes, she wants a belly rub. Other times, she just looks at me for a while, staring up at me with cookie eyes. I bake.

I can feel her thoughts. She wants to know things. One particular night, she wanted to know if I was the only human who thought she was smart and was more than a rescue dog with odd issues. I emphasized the fact that I've bragged about her so many times, my friends consider her a part of the Jones family. Nothing could slow me down now. I told her that her sweet beauty and her charming ways have affected many people, those who understand what it means to love and commit and share their toast. And smart? I rolled my eyes, telling her, "No one is smarter than you or Mojo or Julia. We all have our own unique intelligence, and it has nothing to do with the fact that you don't have a diploma." I think she got it. She wanted a belly rub.

A week later, I had lunch with my friend Marco, who never claims to be psychic, but he is one of the most spirit sensitive people I know. I was eating a spinach salad when one of the leaves, with a particularly long stem, got stuck in my throat. I gagged silently, turning my head, trying to swallow it. At the same time, he said to me, "I have something to say to you. I hope you understand it."

I coughed, dislodging it. "Anything. Tell me anything," I said, grateful to be alive. Marco replied, matter-of-factly. "I cut the stems in half." I wanted to hide under the table. He then said, "Your dog wants to feel appreciated. She also knows that you value and respect her." Spirit can be a heart-stopper.

After five years, I have come to realize how much big feathery paws and strange throaty sounds have altered by life. My dog. Her human. I look at the world upside-down and from different angles, never assuming that what is, will be the same tomorrow. I feel a more vibrant connection to the spiritual realms - one foot planted on spiritual soil. One paw running with angels. I grin at absurd occurrences. I snarl at a noise when it bothers her. I shrug my shoulders when something in the house vanishes forever. I look at a dog and see only a small part of its soul. The remainder of it is somewhere in the cosmos, for the soul is too sprawling and expansive to fit inside one small physical body.

In retrospect, I didn't anticipate that so much of her journey would affect my own, including the amount of strange and intriguing happenings. Insects have now become otherworldly messengers. I was leaning against the back fence, staring at Shaula Pearl, staring at me, when a monarch butterfly flew across the yard and into my face. It kept battering my cheek and my forehead. I had to maneuver it away with my hand, trying not to harm it. It was weird. A few days later, I ran into Julia, of course. She was standing in the metaphysical aisle of a bookstore. She gave me her third eye look, squinting upward. She said to me. "Your mother sent you a hello. It was a butterfly, a monarch."

Thank you God. Thank you Mama. Thank you butterfly. We are all so blessed that Divine Light decided, in lavish amounts of grace, to be accessible to every living being. Also, that we are given a multitude of ways to connect with our souls, and ultimately to find ourselves, our true selves, buried beneath our designer jeans, our jewelry, our face make-up. Shaula Pearl found herself. She linked with her spirit, her individual spirit, for it is everywhere. Spirit is jade green seaweed, tangled on the sand like sea braids. Spirit is dogwood trees, grinning at us with rosy pink blossoms. Spirit lives in a pond with rainbow scaled minnows and fleshy tadpoles, dreaming of legs.

What has struck me deeply, is the magnitude of our interactions with Divine Light, every moment of our lives. If we hug a dog, we hug God. If we kick a dog, we kick God. If we disrespect a dog, we disrespect God. Also, it doesn't matter what you call Divine Light – God. Goddess. Jehovah. Elohim. He-she answers to many names, loving and supporting our souls, exactly the way we entered this life and the way we leave it. We are all children of Divine Light. Shaula Pearl is a glow dog of Divine Light.

Enchantment handed me one more instruction list, supporting the well-being of all souls.

- Number One: Breathe deeply and slowly. A rise in oxygen levels and blood flow can result in a healthy brain.
- Number Two: Meditate with a dog. It increases your IQ and activates your thinking ability.
- Number Three: Think beautiful thoughts. It relieves stress and keeps you disease free.
- Number Four: Be yourself. Follow your own path, not someone else's. Then you will find yourself.

Number Five: Laugh often. It releases endorphins, making you feel joyous.

Number Six: Cry when you feel like it. It increases oxygen levels and cleanses the brain like an internal loofah.

Number Seven: Embrace change. Flow with it like a duck down a stream. New routines make you more flexible and resilient. If Divine Light is guiding you, handing you a paddle, you can't lose.

Number Eight: Follow your own journey. Include others. Make love your religion.

Enchantment will pull out the Egyptian Goddess in you, the strong warrior priestess, the warrior priest. There was the classic knock at my door, late in the evening. I had to laugh. People are always bringing me dessert. One of my dearest friends, Zahara, walked in with her usual princess prance, which I have long admired, and carrying a plate of oatmeal cookies. I forgave her, seeing how there were no chocolate chips in them. We sat down, eager to eat and talk. I introduced my new living room without squirming. I claimed it. It had morphed into its final stage, more of a bohemian look. It was unconventional with a diversity of colors and interesting objects, if you considered paper bags artsy. Also, half the walls were now purple with crows on them – my own joy run.

Zahara sat down, surveying the demolition scene and the art work. "Interesting," she said, studying a sock that was twisting around an arrangement of fake cherry blossoms.

"I'm into abstract art," I responded, clinging to the idea that I was a bohemian goddess. I waited for the cover-up response to my dwelling space, gushing about the good energy or the pretty paper plates.

I was pleasantly surprised. "Yes," she responded. "I can see that. It's so you."

Zahara left an hour later in full prance. She always claimed herself. I got that now. I joined Shaula Pearl in her closet, leaving the sock where it was. Life had become rich and delicious like one mindful bite of chocolate Kahlua cheesecake.

Being in the child care profession, I was in a position to help very needy families with child care, and other pressing issues, such as food and shelter. I had parents who lived in someone's backyard, in a small tent with three children. I had a family who was living out of their car, near a park. Another family was living in a friend's garage with a large mattress for a bed, and rats to help take their minds off the cold. I remember one day, in particular, reminding me to look beneath the surface of things. A young girl, homeless, maybe twenty, came into my office. She looked thirty. Her face was dry and cracked, but her eyes were glowing. She introduced herself as Hannah, and then said, "That's with an H at the beginning and an H at the end." She sounded so sweet and innocent. It was something a four year old might say.

Hannah appeared nervous, glancing at my door. I asked her what was wrong, besides the obvious. She left for a moment and came back with a medium sized dog who reminded me of Wicca. I asked her to stay a while, offering her the plush chair meant for clients. In my head, she was important enough. Then, I said the wrong thing. "If you can't take care of Zoey, I can find her a home. She gave Zoey a quick hug and said, "No thank you. I saw her in someone's backyard, chained to a chair. She was very neglected. They gave her to me. She keeps me sane. We love each other." Love was her glow.

I felt bad that I had suggested what I did. I was concerned for the dogs welfare but had overlooked their relationship, their journey together. Zoey looked fed and happy, and she was better off with Hannah, than whoever it was who didn't get it. I forgave myself with a good lecture, that I wasn't always right and that I wasn't perfect at anything, except brownies, soft in the middle and melting in your mouth with a slight crispiness to the outer layer. The secret's been guarded too long – your favorite brownie mix, fifty stirs around the bowl, clockwise, and then pour in, with no guilt, a goblet full of chocolate chips. Following that, state your intentions. I pour in a verbal blessing. Anyone who swallows a bite, feels joyous and full of abundance. It's easy enchantment, but you have to follow the instructions if you want the desired results, over and over again.

Souls are more difficult. The same formula for enchantment, for everyone, would be unrealistic. Look at the tree of life with its roots, extending to the middle of the earth, and its branches, scraping the sky. It has many paths, all leading to the joy of our own souls. Divine Light is there with us, cheering us on without conditions, to keep moving forward, climbing as high as our dreams take us. The beauty and splendor of our spiritual existence, awaits us. All of us. We are all loved, effortlessly and without reason. Thank you, my sweet dogs. I've learned much from you.

The stars churn above us in the night sky, deep in a divine cauldron, lit with moon-silver ribbons of light and rainbows of nebulous souls, all glowing in the mind of God, in the heart of the Goddess. Purple jacaranda petals cover the ground like lace shawls, and the glint of dragonfly wings, flit across our vision like sprays of miniature jewels. We miss much at times, focused on our bank account or the pain in our shoulder or the stain on our couch. Life is undeniably challenging, but when I look in Shaula Pearl's eyes, I see what it's all about. Love. Joy. Commit to what you love. Joy follows.

Love is the mother of enchantment. She sees all and knows all, for she is spirit. She is soft and lovely and abundantly plush, but she comes with a message. Don't dish it out and then take it away. Shaula Pearl needs the same amount of attention today, as she did five years ago. You have to work it, but it's worth a soul. Her joy is always there, snuggled under her peacock eye, swirling around her paws and riding her big tail. But her memories still haunt her, like a stubborn ghost, rattling his chains around in her closet. You beg him to leave and never come back, but he does, in the early hours, when the deep blues of the night, fade into the pastel dreams of the morning. Shaula Pearl wanders into my room, checking on me. Without warning, she bolts, running down the hallway, thudding into her closet because something scared her.

Life is never going to be perfect for Shaula Pearl. I wish it was. We have a tendency to want everything flawless. It's not our fault. We have eons of spiritual memories, very alive and powerful, echoing our perfected selves. I shred myself up, at times. I like my ears, nose and eyes. Caterpillars are on my joyful encounter list, but not above my eyes, imitating my eyebrows. I don't like my elbows. They look pointy in pictures, and it really bugs me. I like my hands but not my arms. They should be an inch longer. I don't like my hips, but I like my legs and my feet, including my toes, but not my big toe. It looks like a thumb. On the other hand, Shaula Pearl is perfect. I tell her that all the time while I'm rubbing her belly. Sometimes, even now, it stiffens a little. I talk her through it until it softens.

It's hard to imagine my life without her. I try not to think about it, but the day will come. I will cradle her in my arms and cry my heart out. I think about crying. It has nothing to do with my beliefs. I know that she will always be with me, staring at me, poking me in the side and thundering joyously around the house. But when someone we love, passes away, you can't touch them anymore or look at them or share things with them, at least physically - a new hairdo, a plate of cookies or even just a thought. It's more than just missing them. It's an intense and profound sadness. It takes you to a place where you realize how priceless it is to be alive and to be with each other.

When my mother died, I bent over from the waist down and couldn't straighten up for at least twenty minutes. That night, I slept at the end of Rachael's bed, curled up like a dog. Still, I knew she was okay. She sang to me the next day, a song that we always sang together when I was younger. It belted out of homeless women, leaning against a travel agency, where I had just cancelled a flight. The song begins with, Count your blessings, name them one by one.

Shaula Pearl is slowing down. She doesn't jump on my desk anymore. It takes her longer to get up from the carpet. Sometimes, she doesn't eat right away. She might not eat her biscuit, but she places it near her closet and pounces on it. She still claims my socks, plays with paper bags and loves her buffalo. At night, she joy runs, but it's more of a gentle run and not as long. At the end of her joy run, she wants a belly rub to relax. My sweet girl. My enchanted girl.

She is still very ghost-like. She walks on silent paws like a cat. I see her first, out of the corner of my eye, approaching me, as slow as a drip of honey. Sometimes, I don't see her at all. She appears like magic, mainly when I'm writing. If I look at her, she looks away, with or without a camera. Then she looks back at me. My funny girl.

Joy thuds are gone for the most part. No more thrashing around in her closet. She is a cool princess. Now, she's poking me with her nose, one quick, gently poke, with goddess attitude, telling me that I need to relax and pet her. That alone was almost impossible to imagine, our first month together. Almost is a crucial word. It echoes the vibration of hope. Without it, enchantment would have been a pipe dream.

One enchanted day, I woke up early, checking the throw rug at the side of the bed. It was all scrambled up, a sure sign that she had slept there. I didn't get up. Instead, I yelled, "I'm awake!" She came prancing in, sniffing my arm that was dangling over the mattress. A moment later, she took off, twisting around in mid-air and down the hallway. She wasn't barking. It's one of her silent joy runs. I like that. Joy doesn't have to be an intense outburst of wild energy. It can be subtle with a quiet beauty to it. My lovely girl.

Later in the morning, I went in the backyard, searching for sun. I found a small spot, squeezing into it, grateful that I could feel warm when I wanted to. Shaula Pearl was already in her favorite spot, about five yards away, on the wood planks. A sudden breeze blew through the yard, rustling the long palm fronds. She bolted inside. Seconds later, she was back out, walking over to me, staring at me. My brave girl. It took her five years to claim the yard. Also, she claimed her right to receive light. I am astounded by the amount of pictures that support this. Divine Light is making a statement. I'm here. I never leave you.

We had an early dinner together, chatting quietly about the day. We retired early, going upstairs to watch a zombie movie. I grinned. You can sneak a virtuous message into anything. A remarkably brainy zombie was having a conversation with his best friend, who was also a zombie, trying to convince him to look up his old girlfriend. His friend replied, "But I'm dead." The other zombie replied, "That's got nothing to do with it. Love is the most powerful force in the universe." It was a persuasive moment. At the end of the movie, he proposed to his high school sweetheart. She said yes, kissing him passionately. I flinched. I can't judge. People flinch at my carpet.

When the movie ended, I switched off the one overhead lightbulb, leaving the lamp on, near the foot of the bed. I wrote for a few hours. She stayed with me, calculating the jump up. She made it. She looks so peaceful. My enchanted girl.

I fell asleep, writing. My head jerked. I looked over at Shaula Pearl, knowing her next move. She would leave the room, the moment I shut my laptop. My quirky girl. I went to bed, counting my blessings, one by one, and then saying what I always say, loud enough for her to hear me.

I will always say it.

"Good night, Shaula Pearl. I love you. Sweet dreams. Joy forever."

Epilogue to Enchantment

The woods are lovely, dark and deep,
but I have promises to keep and
miles to go before I sleep.
Robert Frost

Joy is such a delicious and delightful word. It makes a whoosh sound like chocolate. Joy has elegant wings like an albatross, riding on wind and airborne dreams, daring this beautiful bird to fly unimaginable distances, thousands of miles, almost effortlessly. What an amazing joy run, not unlike Shaula Pearls. She gathers her power, and on the wind of her soul, she flies, landing only when she is out of breath, for she has traveled miles in her heart.

She lives a magical life now, but she works it daily. Her fears are smashed down, about as far as they will go, but they whisper to her, insisting that they are alive and real. I tell her, they can't hurt her. They have no power over enchanted beings. She believes me, but she has her moments. The night lulls them away. We sit in the yard together on warm evenings. She stares at me. I stare at the stars. I have always felt guided by them. They awaken our souls from an immortal sleep. They sing a melodious message, of the dawn of creation, of selfless acts, of making worlds when you don't have to. They speak of truth, of beauty. They tell you things, besides the course of your path. You can make a difference. You can help. You can make the world better.

You can rescue a soul. You can foster an animal until he's adopted, helping him feel comfortable around people. You can host a chocolate 'animal-rescue' potluck. Ask friends to bring items that you can donate to a shelter such as toys and blankets. You can send beautiful thoughts from any place on the earth – in a work meeting, in a swivel chair or on a walk. One beautiful thought expands the energy of love and healing, rippling it out, affecting the very fiber of all souls. An old basset hound feels it, miles away, and howls. The neighbor, across from you, smiles at nothing. A dog, trembling in fear, feels it, and holds onto that one spark of hope that he will rise above his circumstance. If you feel inspired to, send a beautiful thought to Shaula Pearl. She can never receive enough love, nor can any soul.

Our thoughts are rooted in our imagination. Whatever we imagine, is not a dreamy diversion of our minds. Imagination creates a mental image, full of sounds and colors. Give power to it. Tell your brain it is real and solid. Imagination has gotten you everything you have, creating your reality. It can also create a better reality for others. Imagine dogs being bathed in Divine Light. White light protects. Siphon in colors, vibrating with spiritual energy. Put a flower in your home that reflects that energy, expanding the power of your thoughts, creating beautiful healings. Choose your flowers. These are only suggestions.

Purple vibrates with a richness of nobility and dignity and will surface their inner goddess. Place the gracious power of lavender in your sacred space, a room where you pray or mediate. Dogs will feel its persuasive and gentle power, giving them strength and a sense of their divine nature.

Yellow vibrates with personal power. Place a yellow daisy in the center of your house. It is a stellar color. Let it be the sun, the passion of the sky, illuminating the souls of all those in need. Dogs will vibrate with the power of their will, of celestial light.

Orange is a fire element. It vibrates with joy and courage. Place the warm vibrancy of orange tulips by your bed. They look dreamy, curled up in their cocoon petals. Dogs will feel the dreams of their souls emerging, giving them hope, a strong pulsating hope, healing wounded hearts, supporting emotional balance.

Blue vibrates with calmness and inner peace. Place forget-me-nots in your house. Their soothing aura will help dogs feel less stressed and anxious and that angelic help is with them. It will ease loneliness.

Pink resonates with the energy of health and happiness. Place a zinnia in a room that you love. Its bold and bright aura will sing out – look at me. I am worthy of feeling beautiful and valued. Dogs will feel the love of their creator and your love, also.

White is faith, besides protection. Place a white gardenia in a bowl of water, in your bedroom. Its silky petals will send lovely thoughts to animals in need – a joyful energy long forgotten, the hope of new journeys.

I showed a video, in a human development class, focusing on a crow who was hungry. The crow bent a straight wire into a hook, to get food out of narrow container. At a lunch break, I saw an adult struggling with a juice carton, trying to get the straw into a small hole. We are all equal in our own way, with our own souls, living inside the unique designs of our own bodies.

A year after I adopted Shaula Pearl, I attended a workshop on increasing your own innate psychic abilities. The lady in charge, named Iris, had psychic and medium skills, but she had never connected with animals. During her lecture, on communicating with spirits, she paused, telling us that a brown dog was in the room who was jumping up and down and saying eagerly, "I'm a dog! I'm a dog!" She inquired, if anyone in the audience had ever had a brown lab. I raised my hand, sensing that it was Mesa. It wasn't hard. I was the only one in the room who had ever lost a lab. Besides, all Mesa did, the first seven years of her life, was jump up and down with her rabbits.

I saw Iris a week later, speaking at another workshop. She told me, with much exuberance, that ever since Mesa had appeared to her, she now sees animal spirits all the time, especially in supermarkets, following their families around. She also told me that animals enjoy their shapes, their feathers, their wings, their paws, rabbits in particular. I smiled at that.

I have to give credit to one more psychic, a wonderful and caring lady named Sheila, who communicates with the souls of animals. I was amazed at her accuracy. Shaula Pearl told her that it was quite a journey, finding each other. She told her that she likes it when I meditate. She explained to Sheila that I was working on a project, involving her, and that I needed to release it. Also, she told her that her health was declining, and it was getting harder to get up. She informed her that when she passes, I won't be as sad as I think I will be. I will trust her on that one. She is also my guide, an advanced soul. I figured as much.

At the end of the session, Sheila asked me if I had a question for Shaula Pearl. I did. I wanted to end this book with a message from her, in her own words. I had asked her myself, hearing the word love, but I wanted more. I was thankful for Sheila's abilities, feeling that she had more to say. Shaula Pearl said, "Love and love and love. That's the key."

While I was writing this epilogue, I took a break, doing a yoga stretch at the foot of my bed. It turned into a short meditative session. Shaula Pearl joined me, jumping on the bed. I revamped the lotus position, sitting on my knees, placing my arms on the bed, getting closer to her. She is such good energy. Within seconds, she placed a paw in my hand. My camera was on the floor, a few feet away from my left leg. I stretched it out, trying to shove it closer, so I could reach it with my other hand. I felt like a pretzel, half-twisted, grateful that I had kept my yoga tape out of the garage. I took a picture, not a moment too soon. She knows it. We are all connected. We need to dissolve the illusion that we are separate beings and that one is better than the next.

If I pledge to a team, it is team enchantment. Join me. Take the enchantment pledge. Enchant a soul. Love deeply and with passion, so that your very soul all but flies out of you. Be a doorway to light.

Love and joy to you and to all the animals who need us.

Geila

The Enchantment Pledge

I pledge, as a child of Divine Light, to drink deeply of life, to feel the sun glowing golden within my heart, to feel the moon, pouring into my dreams, telling me who I am, and to hear the stars, whispering to my soul, sharing their infinite vision of my journey. I will merge with the earth. Unite with spirit. Listen for guidance. I am ready.

I am hope. I am love. I am joy. I will vibrate with these luminous energies, sharing them with all souls who are in need of enchantment. I will cast off doubt and be fearless, embracing myself as I am. For then, I can be a light, guiding others to meadows with honey-scented flowers, to safe and beautiful places where they can heal, sensing the treasures of their own souls.

Divine Light. Hear my name. (insert first name.) I pledge to you my never-ending soul, in wild and joyful abundance, to HALO, to heal all life opportunities. I will dismiss no one, knowing that we are all loved equally.

I am a soul healer, now and forever.

So be it.

Printed in the United States
By Bookmasters